Prentice Hall **Realidades** **B**

Leveled Vocabulary and Grammar Workbook
Guided Practice

PEARSON

Boston, Massachusetts   Chandler, Arizona   Glenview, Illinois   Upper Saddle River, New Jersey

Table of Contents

Dear Parents and Guardians:

¡Saludos!

Greetings and welcome to Level B of *Realidades*. Your child has already learned what it is like to be in a foreign language class, just as you have learned how to help your child succeed in this endeavor. Your child has already begun to understand, speak, read, and write Spanish, and explored various Spanish-speaking cultures. No doubt, you and your child have also discovered that language learning is a building process that requires considerable time and practice, but also that it is one of the most rewarding things your child can learn in school.

Language learning calls on all of the senses and on many skills that are not necessarily used in other kinds of learning. Spanish classes may differ from other classes in a variety of ways. For instance, lectures generally play only a small role in the language classroom. Because the goal is to learn to communicate, students interact with each other and with their teacher as they learn to express themselves about things they like to do (and things they don't), their personalities, the world around them, foods, celebrations, pastimes, technology, and much more. Rather than primarily listening to the teacher, reading the text, and memorizing information as they might in a social studies class, language learners will share ideas; discuss similarities and differences between cultures; ask and answer questions; and work with others to practice new words, sounds, and sentence structures. As in Level A, your child will be given a variety of tasks to do in preparation for such an interactive class. He or she will complete written activities, perform listening tasks, watch and listen to videos, and go on the Internet. In addition, to help solidify command of words and structures, time will need to be spent on learning vocabulary and practicing the language until it starts to become second nature. Many students will find that using flash cards and doing written practice will help them become confident using the building blocks of language.

To help you help your child in this endeavor, we offer the following insights into the textbook program your child will be using, along with suggestions for ways that you can help build your child's motivation and confidence—and as a result, success in learning Spanish.

Textbook Organization

Your child is learning Spanish using *Realidades*, which means "realities." The emphasis throughout the text is on learning to use the language in authentic, real ways. Chapters are organized by themes such as food and health, family and celebrations, stores and shopping, etc. Each chapter begins with a section called **A primera vista** (*At First Glance*): **Vocabulario en contexto**, which gives an initial presentation of new grammar and vocabulary in the form of pictures, short dialogues, audio recordings, and video. Once students have been exposed to the new language, the **Manos a la obra** (*Let's Get to Work*): **Vocabulario en uso** and **Gramática y vocabulario en uso** sections offer lots of practice with the language as well as explanations of how the language works. The third section, **¡Adelante!** (*Moving Ahead!*), provides activities for your child to use the language by understanding readings, giving oral or written presentations, and learning more about the cultural perspectives of Spanish speakers. Finally, all chapters conclude with an at-a-glance review of the chapter material called **Repaso del capítulo** (*Chapter Review*), with summary lists and charts, and practice activities like those on the chapter test. If students have trouble with a given task, the **Repaso del capítulo** tells them where in the chapter they can go to review.

Organization of this Workbook

The Guided Practice Activities workbook is designed to be consistent and easy to use. Each chapter consists of three main sections: vocabulary flash cards; vocabulary check sheets; and numbered worksheets to support the grammar, reading task, and oral or written presentation in the chapter.

The vocabulary flash cards review all the vocabulary words listed in the **Repaso del capítulo** (*Chapter Review*) of *Realidades*, Level B. On the picture cards, students write the Spanish vocabulary word in the space provided. On the cards with a printed word or phrase, students copy that Spanish word or phrase in the space provided to practice spelling.

The vocabulary checks are pages designed to be torn out of the workbook for reviewing chapter vocabulary. Students write in Spanish words or their English equivalents and then fold the paper as marked to check their answers.

Finally, the grammar tutorial sheets, which are numbered from 1 to 6, give your child more structured practice than the textbook. The first four activities provide step-by-step review and practice of the main grammar topics in the chapter. The final two activities in each chapter support the reading task and the oral presentation (in the A chapters) and writing presentation (in the B chapters) in the **¡Adelante!** sections of the textbook by focusing students on the steps required to complete the task.

Strategies for Supporting Language Learners

Here are some suggestions that will help your child become a successful language learner.

Routine:

- Provide a special, quiet place for study, equipped with a Spanish-English dictionary, pens or pencils, paper, computer, and any other items your child's teacher suggests.
- Encourage your child to study Spanish at a regular time every day. A study routine will greatly facilitate the learning process.

Strategy:

- Remind your child that class participation and memorization are very important in a foreign language course.
- Tell your child that in reading or listening activities, as well as in the classroom, it is not necessary to understand every word. Suggest that he or she listen or look for key words to get the gist of what's being communicated.
- Encourage your child to ask questions in class if he or she is confused. Remind the child that other students may have the same question. This will minimize frustration and help your child succeed.

Real-life connection:

- Outside of the regular study time, encourage your child to review new words in their proper context as they relate to the chapter themes. For example, when studying the vocabulary for the household chapter, *Capítulo 6B*, have your child help with household chores and ask him or her to name the tasks in Spanish. You could also have your child label household objects with adhesive notes containing the Spanish words. Similarly, while reviewing vocabulary in section 4 of *Para empezar*, have your child bring flash cards for place names on a trip into town and review words for the buildings you pass along the way. If your child can include multiple senses while studying (see the school and say *escuela*, or taste ice cream and say *helado)*, it will help reinforce study and will aid in vocabulary retention.

- Motivate your child with praise for small jobs well done, not just for big exams and final grades. A memorized vocabulary list is something to be proud of!

Resources:

- Offer to help frequently! Your child may have great ideas for how you can facilitate his or her learning experience.

- Ask your child's teacher, or encourage your child to ask, about how to best prepare for and what to expect on tests and quizzes.

- Ask your child's teacher about the availability of audio recordings and videos that support the text. The more your child sees and hears the language, the greater the retention. There are also on-line and CD-ROM based versions of the textbook that may be useful for your child.

- Visit www.realidades.com with your child for more helpful tips and practice opportunities, including downloadable audio files that your child can play at home to practice Spanish. Enter the appropriate Web Code from the list below for the section of the chapter that the class is working on and you will see a menu that lists the available audio files. They can be listened to on a computer or on a personal audio player.

Capítulo	A primera vista: Vocabulario en contexto	Manos a la obra: Vocabulario en uso and Gramática y vocabulario en uso	Repaso
Level A			
Para empezar			jcd-0099
Capítulo 1A	jcd-0187	jcd-0188	jcd-0189
Capítulo 1B	jcd-0197	jcd-0198	jcd-0199
Capítulo 2A	jcd-0287	jcd-0299	jcd-0289
Capítulo 2B	jcd-0297	jcd-0298	jcd-0299
Capítulo 3A	jcd-0387	jcd-0388	jcd-0389
Capítulo 3B	jcd-0397	jcd-0398	jcd-0399
Capítulo 4A	jcd-0487	jcd-0488	jcd-0489
Capítulo 4B	jcd-0497	jcd-0498	jcd-0499
Level B			
Capítulo 5A	jcd-0587	jcd-0588	jcd-0589
Capítulo 5B	jcd-0597	jcd-0598	jcd-0599
Capítulo 6A	jcd-0687	jcd-0688	jcd-0689
Capítulo 6B	jcd-0697	jcd-0698	jcd-0699
Capítulo 7A	jcd-0787	jcd-0788	jcd-0789
Capítulo 7B	jcd-0797	jcd-0798	jcd-0799
Capítulo 8A	jcd-0887	jcd-0888	jcd-0889
Capítulo 8B	jcd-0897	jcd-0898	jcd-0899
Capítulo 9A	jcd-0987	jcd-0988	jcd-0989
Capítulo 9B	jcd-0997	jcd-0998	jcd-0999

Review:

- Encourage your child to review previously learned material frequently, and not just before a test. Remember, learning a language is a building process, and it is important to keep using what you've already learned.

- To aid vocabulary memorization, suggest that your child try several different methods, such as saying words aloud while looking at a picture of the items, writing the words, acting them out while saying them, and so on.

- Suggest that your child organize new material using charts, graphs, pictures with labels, or other visuals that can be posted in the study area. A daily review of those visuals will help keep the material fresh.

- Help your child drill new vocabulary and grammar by using the charts and lists in the **Vocabulario y gramática en uso** and **Repaso del capítulo** sections.

Above all, help your child understand that a language is not acquired overnight. Just as for a first language, there is a gradual process for learning a second one. It takes time and patience, and it is important to know that mistakes are a completely natural part of the process. Remind your child that it took years to become proficient in his or her first language, and that the second one will also take time. Praise your child for even small progress in the ability to communicate in Spanish, and provide opportunities for your child to hear and use the language.

Strategies for Using this Book

At the beginning of a new school year, it is essential to review and practice material regularly so that students do not become frustrated that they have forgotten everything. It is natural to forget, and the best way to get back on track is by frequent review. The activities in this workbook are designed to review and practice material from the *Realidades* textbook and to help students throughout the year.

Here are some tips for helping your child in studying Spanish this year.

Learning vocabulary with flash cards:

Flash cards are a useful tool for learning or reviewing vocabulary. Help your child set up a system for filing material for easy access when reviewing vocabulary, so that he or she can study independently and achieve success. A small box or index card holder can serve as a convenient storage place for the cards. You can stress the importance of organizing words by chapter to keep your child's system coordinated with the textbook.

Your child may want to use the flash card activities in this workbook as models for making his or her own flash cards. If your child is artistic, you can encourage him or her to draw the visualized words as they are done in the Vocabulary Flash Cards section, writing the Spanish word on back of the card instead of below the drawing.

Flash cards are also a useful tool for you to help your child to review vocabulary. You can spend just a few minutes a day going through a handful of cards with your child. If your child has flash cards from Level A, you can use this as an opportunity to prepare for Level B. If your child does not have his or her own flash cards, you may want to encourage him or her to work with a friend.

Supporting reading strategies:

The *Realidades* program provides students with various reading strategies that help them manage what can be a difficult task for some students. Here are some strategies that your child can use in the reading activities in this workbook.

- **Using cognates.** When your child has difficulty with a reading at home, encourage him or her to look for words that are similar to English words in order to help decipher the meaning of the text.

- **Finding meaning using context clues.** If your child stumbles on a word or two in a reading, encourage him or her to use what is written around the word or words to find its meaning. Remind your child that it is not always necessary to know all of the words to understand the meaning of the passage.

- **Using format to find meaning.** Sometimes the title and format of a reading provide a basis for finding meaning in a reading. For example, on pages 240–241 of the Level B textbook, there is a reading about a trip to Peru. By looking at the format of that reading and the pictures, your child should be able to tell that it is a journal and that the person writes each time she is at a different location.

- **Using prior experience.** Often your child's real-life experience can help provide meaning. For example, if your child enjoys shopping and is familiar with the language used in that setting, then the theme **De compras** (*shopping*) will be a familiar setting from which to derive meaning.

Preparing for presentations:

Another way to help your child use these Guided Practice activities is by helping him or her prepare for the oral and written presentations. Of course, the best way to succeed at both is by frequent practice, but here are some pointers to help your child feel more prepared for doing a presentation.

- **Using note cards.** Your child may be allowed to refer to notes when doing an oral presentation, so it is important to have neatly prepared cards. Note cards provide a good way of organizing thoughts before an entire presentation is completed, especially in the case of writing where details tend to be more specific.

- **Using graphic organizers.** Several types of graphic organizers are helpful preparation tools for presentations. Word webs are often used in your child's textbook to organize thoughts and details before a presentation. The textbook often suggests using graphic organizers as a strategy to complete the prewrite step of the writing presentation.

- **Acting it out.** With oral presentations, it is always best to run through the presentation beforehand, so that your child knows what he or she will sound like, and how long the presentation will be.

Don't hesitate to ask your child's teacher for ideas. You will find the teacher eager to help you. You may also be able to help the teacher understand special needs that your child may have, and work together with him or her to find the best techniques for helping your child learn.

Learning to speak another language is one of the most gratifying experiences a person can have. We know that your child will benefit from the effort, and will acquire a skill that will serve to enrich his or her life.

Realidades **B**

Capítulo 5A

Nombre _____

Hora _____

Fecha _____

Vocabulary Flash Cards, Sheet 1

Write the Spanish vocabulary word below each picture. If there is a word or phrase, copy it in the space provided. Be sure to include the article for each noun.

_____

_____

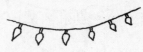

_____

_____

_____

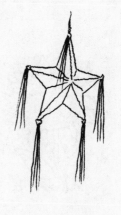

_____

_____

_____

_____

Realidades **B**

Capítulo 5A

Nombre _____

Hora _____

Fecha _____

Vocabulary Flash Cards, Sheet 3

el cumpleaños	el esposo	la esposa
_____ _____	_____ _____	_____ _____

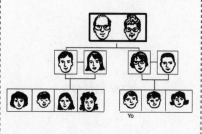 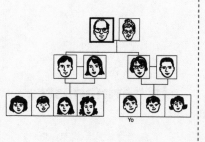 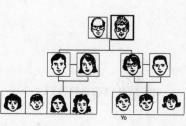

_____ _____	_____ _____	_____ _____

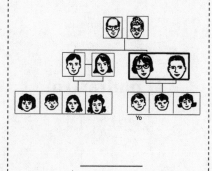 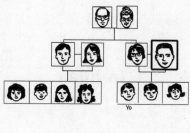 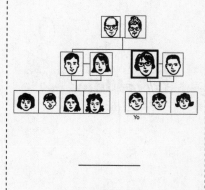

_____ _____	_____ _____	_____ _____

Realidades B

Capítulo 5A

Nombre _____

Hora _____

Fecha _____

Vocabulary Flash Cards, Sheet 4

_____ _____	_____ _____	_____ _____
el hermanastro _____ _____	**la hermanastra** _____ _____	**los hijos** _____ _____
el hijo _____ _____	**la hija** _____ _____	**el padrastro** _____ _____

Realidades Ⓑ

Capítulo 5A

Nombre _____

Hora _____

Fecha _____

Vocabulary Flash Cards, Sheet 5

la madrastra

_____

_____

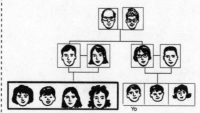

_____

_____

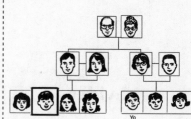

_____

_____

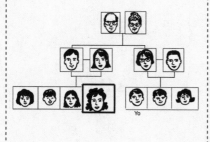

_____

_____

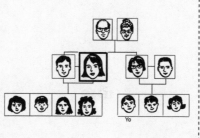

_____

_____

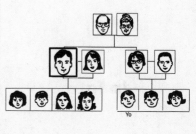

_____

_____

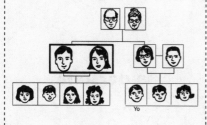

_____

_____

**¡Feliz
cumpleaños!**

_____

_____

celebrar

_____

_____

Realidades B

Capítulo 5A

Nombre _____

Hora _____

Fecha _____

Vocabulary Flash Cards, Sheet 6

el video _the_ _video_	**preparar** _prepare/make_	**sacar fotos** _to take_ _photos_
la foto _the_ _photo_	**que** _what_	**sólo** _only_
mayor, **mayores** _older_	**menor,** **menores** _younger_	**la persona** _the_ _person_

Tear out this page. Write the English words on the lines. Fold the paper along the dotted line to see the correct answers so you can check your work.

el abuelo _____ grandpa (father) _____

la abuela _____ grandma (mother) _____

el hermano _____ brother _____

la hermana _____ sister _____

el hijo _____ son _____

la hija _____ daughter _____

el padre (papá) _____ dad _____

la madre (mamá) _____ mom _____

el primo _____ cousin (male) _____

la prima _____ cousin (female) _____

el tío _____ uncle _____

la tía _____ aunt _____

la persona _____ person _____

el gato _____ cat _____

el perro _____ dog _____

Fold In

Tear out this page. Write the Spanish words on the lines. Fold the paper along
the dotted line to see the correct answers so you can check your work.

grandfather _____

grandmother _____

brother _____

sister _____

son _____

daughter _____

father _____

mother _____

cousin (*male*) _____

cousin (*female*) _____

uncle _____

aunt _____

person _____

cat _____

dog _____

Fold In ◄

Tear out this page. Write the English words on the lines. Fold the paper along the dotted line to see the correct answers so you can check your work.

abrir _____

celebrar _____

decorar _____

hacer un video _____

romper _____

sacar fotos _____

la cámara _____

¡Feliz cumpleaños! _____

_____

los dulces _____

la flor, *pl.* las flores _____

el globo _____

la luz, *pl.* las luces _____

el papel picado _____

_____

el pastel _____

el regalo _____

Fold In

Tear out this page. Write the Spanish words on the lines. Fold the paper along the dotted line to see the correct answers so you can check your work.

to open _____

to celebrate _____

to decorate _____

to videotape _____

to break _____

to take pictures _____

camera _____

Happy birthday! _____

_____

candy _____

flower _____

balloon _____

light _____

cut-paper decorations _____

cake _____

gift, present _____

To hear a complete list of the vocabulary for this chapter, go to www.realidades.com and type in the Web Code jcd-0589. Then click on **Repaso del capítulo.**

Fold In

Realidades B

Capítulo 5A

Nombre _____

Hora _____

Fecha _____

Guided Practice Activities 5A-1

The verb *tener* (p. 42)

- You have already learned some forms of the verb **tener** (*to have*): **tengo, tienes**.
- **Tener** is an irregular verb. Here are its forms.

yo	**tengo**	nosotros/nosotras	**tenemos**
tú	**tienes**	vosotros/vosotras	**tenéis**
usted/él/ella	**tiene**	ustedes/ellos/ellas	**tienen**

A. Write the correct form of **tener** next to each subject pronoun.

1. él _____
2. usted _____
3. ellos _____

4. nosotras _____
5. yo _____
6. tú _____

- **Tener** is used to show relationship or possession.
  Tengo dos hermanas.   *I have two sisters.*
  Tienes una bicicleta.   *You have a bicycle.*

- **Tener** is also used to express age, hunger, and thirst.
  Tengo catorce años.   *I am fourteen years old.*
  Tengo hambre.   *I am hungry.*
  Tengo sed.   *I am thirsty.*

B. Read each numbered sentence with **tener**. Then write the number of that sentence in the correct column in the chart, depending on whether **tener** is used to express possession, age, thirst/hunger, or relationship. Follow the model.

possession	age	thirst/hunger	relationship
	#1		

1. ¿Cuántos años tiene tu tío?
2. Nosotras tenemos diez primos.
3. ¿Tiene sed tu padre?

4. Mi hermana tiene tres años.
5. Yo tengo un regalo para mi abuela.
6. Mis primos tienen mucha hambre.

C. Now look at the following sentences and write in the missing forms of **tener**.

1. Mi prima Ana _____ once años.

2. Yo _____ un regalo para mi tía.

3. Mis hermanos _____ mucha hambre.

4. Nosotros _____ tres gatos.

5. ¿Cuántos años _____ tu padre?

6. ¿ _____ sed tu hermano?

• Web Code: jcd-0504

D. Look at the family tree. Write forms of **tener** to complete each sentence below it.

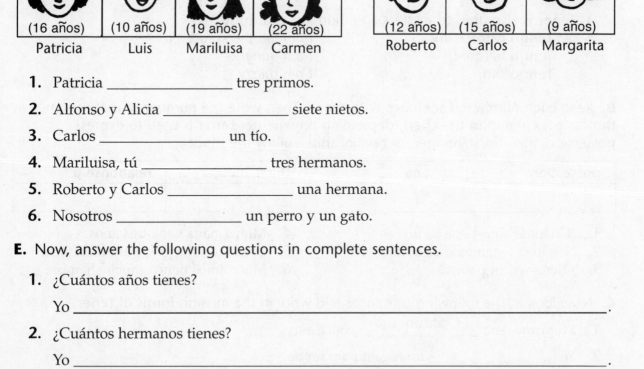

1. Patricia _____ tres primos.

2. Alfonso y Alicia _____ siete nietos.

3. Carlos _____ un tío.

4. Mariluisa, tú _____ tres hermanos.

5. Roberto y Carlos _____ una hermana.

6. Nosotros _____ un perro y un gato.

E. Now, answer the following questions in complete sentences.

1. ¿Cuántos años tienes?

   Yo _____.

2. ¿Cuántos hermanos tienes?

   Yo _____.

3. ¿Tienes sed?

   Sí / No, _____.

4. ¿Tienes hambre?

   Sí / No, _____.

realidades.com Ⓥ
• Web Code: jcd-0504

Realidades **B**

Capítulo 5A

Nombre _____

Fecha _____

Hora _____

Guided Practice Activities 5A-3

Possessive adjectives (p. 48)

- Possessive adjectives are used to indicate who owns what and to show relationships.
- In English, *my*, *your*, *his*, *her*, *our*, and *their* are possessive adjectives.

yo	**mi/mis**	nosotros nosotras	**nuestro/nuestros** **nuestra/nuestras**
tú	**tu/tus**	vosotros vosotras	**vuestro/vuestros** **vuestra/vuestras**
usted/él/ella	**su/sus**	ustedes/ellos/ellas	**su/sus**

- Spanish possessive adjectives, just like other adjectives, change their endings to reflect number. The **nosotros** and **nosotras** forms (**nuestro, nuestra, nuestros, nuestras**) also change to reflect gender.

> **mi** herman**o** / **mis** herman**os**   BUT:
> **mi** hija / **mis** hijas   nuestr**o** tí**o** / nuestr**os** tí**os**
> **tu** flor / **tus** flor**es**   nuestr**a** tí**a** / nuestr**as** tí**as**

A. Look at each noun. Write **S** if the noun is singular and **P** if it is plural.

1. _____ primo

2. _____ regalos

3. _____ hijas

4. _____ flor

5. _____ pastel

6. _____ tío

7. _____ globos

8. _____ familias

B. Now, circle the correct possessive adjective for each of the nouns from **part A**.

1. (**mi** / **mis**) primo

2. (**su** / **sus**) regalos

3. (**tu** / **tus**) hijas

4. (**mi** / **mis**) flor

5. (**tu** / **tus**) pastel

6. (**mi** / **mis**) tío

7. (**su** / **sus**) globos

8. (**tu** / **tus**) familias

C. Write **mi** in front of each singular noun and **mis** in front of each plural noun.

1. _____ piñata

2. _____ hermanos

3. _____ regalos

4. _____ flores

Realidades B

Capítulo 5A

Nombre _____

Hora _____

Fecha _____

Guided Practice Activities 5A-4

Possessive adjectives *(continued)*

D. Look at each noun. Circle **S** if it is singular and **P** if it is plural. Circle **M** if it is masculine and **F** if it is feminine. Follow the model.

Modelo   pasteles   (S /(P)) and ((M)/ F)

1. decoraciones   (S / P) and (M / F)   **4.** flores   (S / P) and (M / F)

2. hijos   (S / P) and (M / F)   **5.** luz   (S / P) and (M / F)

3. gato   (S / P) and (M / F)   **6.** globos   (S / P) and (M / F)

E. Below are the nouns from **part D**. Write **nuestro, nuestra, nuestros,** or **nuestras** in front of each one. Follow the model.

Modelo   _nuestros_   pasteles

1. _____ decoraciones   **4.** _____ flores

2. _____ hijos   **5.** _____ luz

3. _____ gato   **6.** _____ globos

F. Circle the correct word to complete each sentence.

1. Tenemos (**nuestros / nuestras**) decoraciones en el coche.

2. Voy a la fiesta con (**mi / mis**) abuelos.

3. Aquí tienes (**tu / tus**) regalo.

4. Alicia va a hacer una piñata con (**su / sus**) hermano.

5. (**Nuestro / Nuestra**) familia saca muchas fotos en las fiestas.

6. Ella va a la fiesta con (**su / sus**) perro.

G. Write the correct form of the possessive adjective indicated to complete each sentence. Follow the models.

Modelos   nuestro: Ella es   _nuestra_   tía.

          mi: Roberto y Luis son   _mis_   primos.

1. tu: Elena y Margarita son _____ hermanas.

2. mi: León es _____ perro.

3. nuestro: Ellos son _____ primos.

4. su: Adela es _____ abuela.

5. su: Adela y Hernando son _____ abuelos.

6. nuestro: Roberto es _____ hijo.

7. nuestro: Lidia y Susana son _____ tías.

realidades.com

• Web Code: jcd-0505

Lectura: ¡Te invitamos a nuestra miniteca! (pp. 54–55)

A. Part of the reading in your textbook is an invitation to a special celebration. Before skimming the reading, write four pieces of information you would expect to find on an invitation to such a party.

1. _____

2. _____

3. _____

4. _____

Felipe Rivera López
y Guadalupe Treviño Ibarra
esperan el honor de su asistencia
el sábado, 15 de mayo de 2004
para celebrar los quince años de su hija
María Teresa Rivera Treviño.

B. Read through the text of the first part of the invitation (top right). Complete the following.

1. Circle the day of the week in the paragraph above.

2. Underline the date of the party.

3. What is the daughter's full name? _____

_____

Misa
a las cuatro de la tarde
Iglesia Nuestra Señora de Guadalupe
2374 Avenida Linda Vista, San Diego, California
Recepción y cena-baile a las seis de la tarde
Restaurante Luna
7373 Calle Florida, San Diego, California

C. Now, read the second part of the invitation and answer the questions below.

1. Write the times that each of the following takes place:

   (a) the Mass _____ **(b)** the reception _____

2. What will people be doing at the reception? _____

3. At what kind of place will the reception be held? _____

D. Now look back at **part A**. Did you find all of the information you were looking for in the reading? Fill in the simple facts of the reception below.

For whom: _____

Time: _____

Date: _____

Location: _____

realidades.com
• Web Code: jcd-0506

Presentación oral (p. 56)

Task: Pretend you are living with a host family in Chile. They want to know about your family back home. Show them photographs of two family members and talk about the people shown.

A. You will need to have brought in two family photos or "created" photos from an imaginary family by using pictures from a magazine. Use the chart below to organize what you want to say about each person. Follow the model and write similar information about your family members.

Nombre	Es mi...	Edad	Actividad favorita
Isabel	hermana menor	9 años	le gusta cantar

B. Since you will be presenting the information above orally, you will need to put everything into complete sentences. Read the model below to get you started. Be sure to practice speaking clearly when you read the model.

|| *Se llama Isabel. Ella es mi hermana menor. Tiene nueve años.* ||
|| *A Isabel le gusta cantar. Es muy artística.* ||

C. Fill in the spaces below with the information you gathered from **part A**. Make sure you provide all the information you listed about each person.

Person 1: Se llama _____. (**Él / Ella**) es mi _____.

Tiene _____ años. A _____ le gusta _____.

Es _____.

Person 2: Se llama _____. (**Él / Ella**) es mi _____.

Tiene _____ años. A _____ le gusta _____.

Es _____.

D. Practice your presentation with the photos.
   Remember to:

_____ provide all the information on each family member.
_____ use complete sentences.
_____ speak clearly.

Realidades B

Capítulo 5B

Nombre _____

Hora _____

Fecha _____

Vocabulary Flash Cards, Sheet 1

Write the Spanish vocabulary word below each picture. If there is a word or phrase, copy it in the space provided. Be sure to include the article for each noun.

Realidades **B**

Capítulo 5B

Nombre _____ Hora _____

Fecha _____ **Vocabulary Flash Cards, Sheet 2**

_____

_____

_____

_____

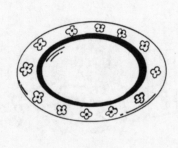

_____

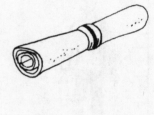

_____

_____

_____

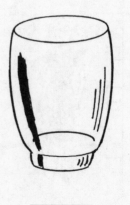

_____

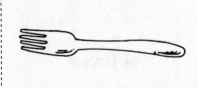

_____

_____

_____

_____

_____

traer

_____

_____

_____

el plato principal

_____

corto, corta	**guapo, guapa**	**el joven**
_____ , _____	_____ , _____	_____ _____
la joven	**el pelo**	**canoso**
_____ _____	_____ _____	_____
castaño	**negro**	**rubio**
_____	_____	_____

pelirrojo, pelirroja

_____,

----

delicioso, deliciosa

_____,

----

desear

_____

pedir

_____

rico, rica

_____,

_____

Me falta(n)...

_____

Quisiera...

_____

ahora

_____

¿Algo más?

_____

_____

Realidades **B**

Capítulo 5B

Nombre _____

Fecha _____

Hora _____

Vocabulary Flash Cards, Sheet 6

De nada.

_____

_____

otro,
otra

_____ ,

_____

¿Me trae...?

_____

_____

Le traigo...

_____

_____

¡Qué...!

_____

_____

largo,
larga

_____

_____

yo
traigo

_____

_____

el joven

_____

_____

de postre

_____

_____

Tear out this page. Write the English words on the lines. Fold the paper along the dotted line to see the correct answers so you can check your work.

el hombre　　_____

la mujer　　_____

corto, corta　　_____

joven　　_____

largo, larga　　_____

viejo, vieja　　_____

el pelo　　_____

canoso　　_____

castaño　　_____

negro　　_____

rubio　　_____

pelirrojo,
pelirroja　　_____

desear　　_____

pedir　　_____

el plato
principal　　_____

Fold In ←

Realidades B

Capítulo 5B

Nombre

Hora

Fecha

Vocabulary Check, Sheet 2

Tear out this page. Write the Spanish words on the lines. Fold the paper along the dotted line to see the correct answers so you can check your work.

man _____

woman _____

short (length) _____

young _____

long _____

old _____

hair _____

gray _____

brown (chestnut) _____

black _____

blond _____

red-haired _____

_____

to want _____

to order _____

main dish _____

_____

Fold In

Realidades B

Capítulo 5B

Nombre

Hora

Fecha

Vocabulary Check, Sheet 3

Tear out this page. Write the English words on the lines. Fold the paper along the dotted line to see the correct answers so you can check your work.

el postre _____

rico, rica _____

el azúcar _____

la cuchara _____

el cuchillo _____

la pimienta _____

el plato _____

la sal _____

la servilleta _____

la taza _____

el tenedor _____

el vaso _____

el camarero _____

la camarera _____

la cuenta _____

el menú _____

Fold In

Realidades **B**

Capítulo 5B

Nombre _____

Hora _____

Fecha _____

Vocabulary Check, Sheet 4

Tear out this page. Write the Spanish words on the lines. Fold the paper along the dotted line to see the correct answers so you can check your work.

dessert _____

rich, tasty _____

sugar _____

spoon _____

knife _____

pepper _____

plate, dish _____

salt _____

napkin _____

cup _____

fork _____

glass _____

waiter _____

waitress _____

bill _____

menu _____

Fold In

To hear a complete list of the vocabulary for this chapter, go to www.realidades.com and type in the Web Code jcd-0599. Then click on **Repaso del capítulo.**

Realidades B

Capítulo 5B

Nombre _____

Hora _____

Fecha _____

Guided Practice Activities 5B-1

The verb *venir* (p. 76)

- The forms of **venir** are similar to the forms of **tener** that you just learned. Notice that the **yo** forms of both verbs end in **-go**.

yo	**vengo**	nosotros/nosotras	**venimos**
tú	**vienes**	vosotros/vosotras	**venís**
usted/él/ella	**viene**	ustedes/ellos/ellas	**vienen**

A. Circle all the forms of **venir** you see in this conversation.

RAÚL: ¿Vienes a la fiesta?

ANA: Si, vengo a las ocho y media.

Mis padres vienen también.

RAÚL: Muy bien. Mis amigos no vienen, pero mi hermano sí viene.

ANA: ¿Cuándo vienen?

RAÚL: Venimos a las nueve.

B. Now, write the forms of **venir** that you circled in **part A** in the correct row of the table. Write only one form of **venir** for each subject pronoun. The first one has been done for you.

Subject pronoun	Form of *venir*
1. yo	
2. tú	*Vienes*
3. usted/él/ella	
4. nosotros	
5. ustedes/ellos/ellas	

C. Complete the following conversation by circling the correct forms of **venir**.

ISABEL: ¿(**Vienes / Vienen**) ustedes a la fiesta?

MÍA: Sí, Marcos y yo (**vienen / venimos**). Pero Luis no (**vienes / viene**).

ISABEL: ¿Por qué no (**viene / vengo**) Luis?

MÍA: Tiene que trabajar. ¿(**Venimos / Vienes**) tú?

ISABEL: Sí. (**Vengo / Vienen**) a las ocho.

MÍA: ¡Qué bien! Nosotros (**venimos / vienes**) a las ocho también.

Realidades **B**

Capítulo 5B

Nombre _____

Hora _____

Fecha _____

Guided Practice Activities 5B-2

• **Venir** is used to say that someone is coming to a place or an event.

D. Write forms of **venir** to say when people are coming to the party.

1. Nosotras _____ a las ocho y cuarto.

2. Tú _____ a las nueve menos cuarto.

3. Elena y Olga _____ a las nueve y media.

4. Yo _____ a las ocho.

5. Marcos _____ a las diez y cuarto.

6. Usted _____ a las diez menos cuarto.

7. Ustedes _____ a las diez.

E. This agenda shows when people have appointments. Complete each sentence to say when each person is coming. Follow the model.

| Modelo | _La Sra. Ramos viene_ a las ocho y media. |

```
8:00
     8:30 La Sra. Ramos
4:00
     Marta
10:00 Raúl y Josefina
11:00 10:45 Yo
      11:30 tú
12:00 Carmen y yo
      Pedro
1:00
2:00
     2:30 Roberto y tú
3:00
     3:30 Lucía y Ramón
4:00
5:00
```

1. _____ a las nueve.

2. _____ a las diez.

3. _____ a las once menos cuarto.

4. _____ a las once y media.

5. _____ a las doce.

6. _____ a la una.

7. _____ a las dos y media.

8. _____ a las tres y media.

F. Answer each question by completing the sentences. Follow the model.

| Modelo | ¿A qué hora vienes a la clase de español? |

Yo ___vengo___ a la clase de español ___a las diez y media___ .

1. ¿A qué hora vienes a la escuela?

Yo _____ a la escuela _____.

2. ¿A qué hora vienes a la clase de español?

Yo _____ a la clase de español _____.

3. ¿A qué hora vienes a casa?

Yo _____ a casa _____.

Realidades **B**

Capítulo 5B

Nombre _____

Fecha _____

Hora _____

Guided Practice Activities 5B-3

The verbs *ser* and *estar* (p. 78)

- There are two Spanish verbs that mean "to be": **ser** and **estar**.
- Review their forms in the present tense.

ser			
yo	**soy**	nosotros/nosotras	**somos**
tú	**eres**	vosotros/vosotras	**sois**
usted/él/ella	**es**	ustedes/ellos/ellas	**son**

estar			
yo	**estoy**	nosotros/nosotras	**estamos**
tú	**estás**	vosotros/vosotras	**estáis**
usted/él/ella	**está**	ustedes/ellos/ellas	**están**

A. Circle the form of **ser** or **estar** that is used in each sentence.

1. Mi madre es profesora.

2. Ellas son de México.

3. Las decoraciones están en mi casa.

4. Nosotras somos artísticas.

5. Yo estoy enferma.

6. Los libros están en la mesa.

7. Tú estás en la oficina.

8. Yo soy la prima de Ana.

B. Look at the forms of **ser** and **estar** that you circled in **part A**. Decide why **ser** or **estar** was used in each. Write the reason using the chart in the explanation on page 258 in your textbook to find the reason why **ser** or **estar** was used in each sentence. Write each reason in the right-hand side of the chart. The first one has been done for you.

Forms of *ser* and *estar*	Reason
1. *es*	*who a person is*
2.	
3.	
4.	
5.	
6.	
7.	
8.	

Realidades **B**

Nombre _____

Hora _____

Capítulo 5B

Fecha _____

Guided Practice Activities 5B-4

The verbs *ser* and *estar (continued)*

C. Circle the correct form of the verb **ser** in each sentence.

1. Mis padres (**son / somos**) profesores.

2. Yo (**soy / eres**) muy atrevida.

3. La comida (**es / eres**) de un restaurante.

D. Circle the correct form of the verb **estar** in each sentence.

1. Tú (**estoy / estás**) muy cansado hoy.

2. La computadora (**está / estamos**) en la oficina.

3. Nosotros (**estamos / están**) muy ocupados.

E. Circle the correct form of **ser** or **estar** in these sentences. Look back at the chart with the uses of **ser** and **estar** if you need help.

1. Mis abuelos (**son / están**) profesores de matemáticas.

2. Yo (**soy / estoy**) enfermo hoy.

3. Tú (**eres / estás**) en la clase de historia.

4. Tomás (**es / está**) de Argentina.

5. Ustedes (**son / están**) argentinos también.

6. Nosotras (**somos / estamos**) muy cansadas.

7. Los libros (**son / están**) muy interesantes.

8. Los libros (**son / están**) en la biblioteca.

F. Write the correct form of **ser** or **estar** to complete each sentence.

1. Tú _____ en la oficina.

2. Nosotras _____ muy ocupadas hoy.

3. Yo _____ estudiante.

4. Mi padre _____ profesor.

5. El video _____ interesante.

6. Los videos _____ en la biblioteca.

7. Nosotros _____ de Guatemala.

8. Tú _____ muy simpático.

realidades.com

• Web Code: jcd-0514

Lectura: Una visita a Santa Fe (pp. 84–85)

A. The reading in your textbook is about the city of Santa Fe. What kinds of information would you expect to find in such a reading? List three ideas below.

1. _____

2. _____

3. _____

B. As you skim the reading you will come across some new cognates. Write the English word for each Spanish cognate listed below.

1. visita _____ 4. típica _____

2. historia _____ 5. histórico _____

3. museo _____ 6. tradicional _____

C. Did you find some activities when you skimmed the reading? If not, look again to find three activities that the cousins are going to do during their visit to Santa Fe. Write the three activities in Spanish below.

1. _____

2. _____

3. _____

D. Now, read the paragraph below from your textbook and answer the questions in English that follow.

> *Durante los días de su visita, el Rancho va a celebrar "un fandango", un baile histórico y típico, con una cena tradicional. Toda la comida es riquísima, pero nuestro plato favorito es el chile con carne y queso. Después de comer, vamos a bailar.*

1. What is a "fandango"? _____

2. What kind of meal will they have to accompany the "fandango"?

   _____

3. What is their favorite dish at the restaurant? _____

4. Which comes first, the meal or dancing? _____

Realidades B

Capítulo 5B

Nombre _____

Hora _____

Fecha _____

Guided Practice Activities 5B-6

Presentación escrita (p. 87)

Task: Pretend your town needs a Spanish-language community guide for restaurants written. Write a review of your favorite local restaurant in Spanish.

❶ Prewrite. Compile the information you will need in order to write about your favorite restaurant. Fill in the information on the lines next to each category.

1. nombre _____

2. descripción general _____
   _____

3. platos principales _____

4. postres _____

❷ Draft.

A. In order to prepare your first draft, write sentences with the information you compiled in **section 1** (**Prewrite**).

1. El restaurante se llama _____.

2. Es un restaurante _____ con
   _____.

3. Los _____ son riquísimos.

4. Hay _____, _____ y _____ también.

B. Read the model below to give you an idea of what a complete review could look like.

> *Café Beló es un café tranquilo con un ambiente intelectual donde puedes pasar el tiempo en la compañía de un buen amigo o un buen libro. Los precios son baratos. Puedes comer un sándwich, una ensalada, un postre o simplemente beber un café. Los postres son riquísimos. Un "plus" es la presentación de grupos musicales los fines de semana.*

C. Use the sentences you wrote in **part A** above and add anything useful from the model to construct your complete review.

❸ Revise. Read through your review. Then you will share it with a partner. You should each check for:

_____ adjective agreement (masculine words with masculine endings, feminine words with feminine endings)

_____ correct use of verb forms

_____ correct spelling

_____ persuasiveness of your review

Realidades B

Capítulo 6A

Nombre _____

Fecha _____

Hora _____

Vocabulary Flash Cards, Sheet 1

Write the Spanish vocabulary word below each picture. If there is a word or phrase, copy it in the space provided. Be sure to include the article for each noun.

_____

_____

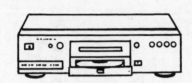

_____

_____

_____

_____

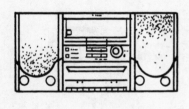

_____

_____

_____

_____

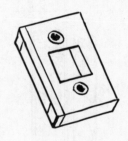

_____

_____

_____

_____

_____

_____

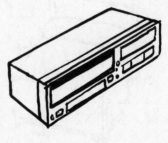

_____

_____

¿De qué color...?

_____ _____

gris

_____

los colores

_____

azul

_____

marrón

_____

amarillo, amarilla

_____,

_____

blanco, blanca

_____,

_____

morado, morada

_____,

_____

Realidades B

Capítulo 6A

Nombre _____

Fecha _____

Hora _____

Vocabulary Flash Cards, Sheet 4

rojo, roja _____, _____	**anaranjado, anaranjada** _____, _____	**importante** _____
rosado, rosada _____, _____	**feo, fea** _____, _____	**mismo, misma** _____, _____
verde _____	**grande** _____	**pequeño, pequeña** _____, _____

propio, propia _____ _____	**el/la mejor** _____ _____	**la cosa** _____ _____
a la derecha (de) _____ _____ _____	**menos... que** _____ _____	**para mí** _____ _____
a la izquierda (de) _____ _____ _____	**el/la peor** _____ _____	**para ti** _____ _____

Realidades B

Capítulo 6A

Nombre _____

Fecha _____

Hora _____

Vocabulary Flash Cards, Sheet 6

el
dormitorio

_____

_____

la
posesión

_____

_____

bonito,
bonita

_____,

_____

poder

_____

_____

los/las
mejores

_____

_____

mejor(es)
que

_____

_____

negro,
negra

_____

_____

los/las
peores

_____

_____

peor(es)
que

_____

_____

Realidades **B**

Capítulo 6A

Nombre

Fecha

Hora

Vocabulary Check, Sheet 1

Tear out this page. Write the English words on the lines. Fold the paper along the dotted line to see the correct answers so you can check your work.

la alfombra _____

el armario _____

la cama _____

la cómoda _____

las cortinas _____

el cuadro _____

el despertador _____

el dormitorio _____

el espejo _____

el estante _____

_____

la lámpara _____

la mesita _____

la pared _____

el equipo de
sonido _____

el lector DVD _____

el televisor _____

la videocasetera _____

Fold In

Tear out this page. Write the Spanish words on the lines. Fold the paper along the dotted line to see the correct answers so you can check your work.

rug _____

closet _____

bed _____

dresser _____

curtains _____

painting _____

alarm clock _____

bedroom _____

mirror _____

shelf,
bookshelf _____

lamp _____

night table _____

wall _____

sound (stereo)
system _____

DVD player _____

television set _____

VCR _____

Fold In →

Realidades B

Capítulo 6A

Nombre _____

Hora _____

Fecha _____

Vocabulary Check, Sheet 3

Tear out this page. Write the English words on the lines. Fold the paper along the dotted line to see the correct answers so you can check your work.

amarillo, amarilla _____

anaranjado, anaranjada _____

azul _____

blanco, blanca _____

gris _____

marrón _____

morado, morada _____

rojo, roja _____

rosado, rosada _____

verde _____

bonito, bonita _____

feo, fea _____

grande _____

importante _____

mismo, misma _____

pequeño, pequeña _____

Fold In

Realidades **B**

Capítulo 6A

Nombre _____

Hora _____

Fecha _____

Vocabulary Check, Sheet 4

Tear out this page. Write the Spanish words on the lines. Fold the paper along
the dotted line to see the correct answers so you can check your work.

yellow _____

_____

orange _____

_____

blue _____

white _____

gray _____

brown _____

purple _____

red _____

pink _____

green _____

pretty _____

ugly _____

large _____

important _____

same _____

small _____

_____

To hear a complete list of the vocabulary for this chapter,
go to www.realidades.com and type in the Web Code jcd-0689.
Then click on **Repaso del capítulo.**

Fold In

Making comparisons (p. 106)

- Use **más** + adjective + **que** to compare two people, things, or actions:

    El libro es **más interesante que** el video.

    *The book is **more interesting than** the video.*

- Use **menos** + adjective + **que** to compare two people, things, or actions:

    Correr es **menos divertido que** montar en bicicleta.

    *Running is **less fun than** riding a bike.*

A. Below are six comparisons. Write a + (plus sign) next to the ones that give the idea of "greater than" or "more than." Write a – (minus sign) next to the ones that give the idea of "worse than" or "less than." Follow the models.

Modelos   más simpático que   __+__

           menos ordenada que   __–__

1. menos divertido que _____   **4.** más interesante que _____

2. más simpático que _____   **5.** menos paciente que _____

3. más reservada que _____   **6.** menos atrevida que _____

B. The sentences below are marked with a + (plus sign) or a – (minus sign). Write in **más** if there is a + and **menos** if there is a –.

1. + El perro es _____ simpático que el gato.

2. – Luisa es _____ artística que Beatriz.

3. – Tomás es _____ trabajador que Marcos.

4. + La bicicleta es _____ grande que el monopatín.

- Some adjectives have special forms for comparisons. See the chart below.

Adjective		Comparative	
bueno / buena	*good*	**mejor (que)**	*better than*
malo / mala	*bad*	**peor (que)**	*worse than*
viejo / vieja	*old*	**mayor (que)**	*older than*
joven	*young*	**menor (que)**	*younger than*

C. Choose the correct comparative to complete each sentence.

1. Lorena tiene catorce años. Lidia tiene quince años. Lorena es (**mayor / menor**) que Lidia.

2. El restaurante grande es malo. El restaurante pequeño es bueno. El restaurante grande es (**mejor / peor**) que el restaurante pequeño.

3. Mi abuela tiene sesenta años. Tu abuela tiene cincuenta y ocho años. Mi abuela es (**mayor / menor**) que tu abuela.

Realidades B

Capítulo 6A

Nombre _____

Fecha _____

Hora _____

Guided Practice Activities 6A-2

The superlative (p. 110)

- To say someone or something is the *most* or the *least*:

    el / la / los / las + noun + **más / menos** + adjective

    Es **el libro más interesante** de la biblioteca.

- To say someone or something is the *best* or the *worst*:

    el / la / los / las + mejor(es) / peor(es) + noun

    Es **el peor libro** de la biblioteca.

A. Below are eight superlative expressions. Write a + (plus sign) next to the ones that give the idea of the *most* or the *best*. Write a – (minus sign) next to the ones that give the idea of the *least* or the *worst*.

1. la lámpara más grande _____

2. la mesita más fea _____

3. el peor video _____

4. las mejores cortinas _____

5. el espejo menos feo _____

6. la alfombra menos bonita _____

7. los peores cuadros _____

8. los mejores despertadores _____

B. Look at each sentence and see whether it is marked with a + or a –. Write in **más** if there is a + and **menos** if there is a –.

1. + Mi tío es la persona _____ simpática de mi familia.

2. – La cama es la _____ grande de todas.

3. – Marzo es el mes _____ bonito del año.

4. + Sandra es la persona _____ divertida de la familia.

C. Choose the correct superlative to complete each sentence. Circle the word you have chosen.

1. Me gusta mucho nadar y montar en bicicleta. Para mí, julio es el (**mejor / peor**) mes del año.

2. Todos mis primos son inteligentes, pero Alberto es el (**más / menos**) inteligente de todos. Es muy estudioso y trabajador también.

3. Me gusta mucho esquiar. Para mí, julio es el (**mejor / peor**) mes del año.

4. No me gustan los libros aburridos. Tu libro es el (**más / menos**) aburrido de todos. Es bastante interesante.

5. Mis abuelos son muy divertidos. Son las personas (**más / menos**) divertidas de la familia.

6. No me gusta esta cama. Es la cama (**más / menos**) grande de la casa.

realidades.com

- Web Code: jcd-0604

Stem-changing verbs: *poder* and *dormir* (p. 112)

- **Poder** (*to be able to do something*) and **dormir** (*to sleep*) are both stem-changing verbs like **jugar**, which you learned previously. Just like **jugar**, only the **nosotros/ nosotras** and **vosotros/vosotras** forms of **poder** and **dormir** do not change their stems.

- Here are the forms of **poder** and **dormir**:

yo	puedo	nosotros/nosotras	podemos
tú	puedes	vosotros/vosotras	podéis
usted/él/ella	puede	ustedes/ellos/ellas	pueden

yo	duermo	nosotros/nosotras	dormimos
tú	duermes	vosotros/vosotras	dormís
usted/él/ella	duerme	ustedes/ellos/ellas	duermen

A. Circle the forms of **poder** and **dormir** in each sentence. Then underline the stem in each verb you circled. The first one has been done for you.

1. (Dormimos) ocho horas al día.
2. ¿Puedes montar en bicicleta?
3. No puedo trabajar hoy.
4. Mis hermanos duermen mucho.

5. Podemos traer la comida.
6. Duermo mucho los fines de semana.
7. No podemos hablar francés.
8. Ud. duerme en una cama grande.

B. Now, write the words you circled in **part A** next to each subject pronoun below.

1. nosotros _____
2. tú _____
3. yo _____
4. ellos _____

5. nosotros _____
6. yo _____
7. nosotros _____
8. Ud. _____

C. Circle the correct form of **poder** or **dormir** to complete each sentence.

1. Mis amigos y yo (**dormimos** / **duermen**) diez horas al día.
2. Roberto no (**puedo** / **puede**) ir a la fiesta.
3. Ustedes (**dormimos** / **duermen**) en la cama más grande de la casa.
4. Tú y yo (**puedes** / **podemos**) traer unos discos compactos.
5. Linda y Natalia (**duermo** / **duermen**) en un dormitorio grande.
6. Nosotros no (**podemos** / **puedes**) usar el lector DVD.
7. Tú (**dormimos** / **duermes**) en el dormitorio con la alfombra azul.

Realidades B

Capítulo 6A

Nombre

Fecha

Hora

Guided Practice Activities 6A-4

Stem-changing verbs: *poder* and *dormir (continued)*

D. Complete the sentences with forms of **poder** and **dormir**. Follow the models.

Modelos Paco (**poder**) ir a la biblioteca.

Paco ___*puede*___ ir a la biblioteca.

Mónica (**dormir**) en el dormitorio grande.

Mónica ___*duerme*___ en el dormitorio grande.

1. Olivia (**poder**) montar en monopatín.

   Olivia _____ montar en monopatín.

2. Javier (**dormir**) ocho horas al día.

   Javier _____ ocho horas al día.

3. Tú (**dormir**) en un dormitorio con tu hermano.

   Tú _____ en un dormitorio con tu hermano.

4. Yo (**poder**) usar la videocasetera.

   Yo _____ usar la videocasetera.

5. Nosotros (**poder**) comprar unas cortinas para el dormitorio.

   Nosotros _____ comprar unas cortinas para el dormitorio.

6. Nosotros (**dormir**) en un dormitorio pequeño.

   Nosotros _____ en un dormitorio pequeño.

7. Ustedes (**dormir**) mucho los fines de semana.

   Ustedes _____ mucho los fines de semana.

E. Write sentences about yourself and your friends using forms of **poder**. Follow the models. Use ideas from the list or other words you know.

> **montar en bicicleta / esquiar / patinar / montar en monopatín /
> hablar español / nadar / patinar / tocar la guitarra / jugar a ¿...?**

Modelos Yo ___*puedo montar en bicicleta*___.

Mis amigos y yo ___*podemos nadar*___.

1. Yo _____.

2. Yo no _____.

3. Mis amigos y yo _____.

4. Mis amigos y yo no _____.

realidades.com

• Web Code: jcd-0605

Realidades Ⓑ

Capítulo 6A

Nombre _____

Fecha _____

Hora _____

Guided Practice Activities 6A-5

Lectura: El desastre en mi dormitorio (pp. 116–117)

A. Try to guess the meaning of the following cognates. If you are having difficulty, skim through the reading in your textbook to find these words in context. Write your answers in the spaces below.

1. desastre _____
2. posesiones _____
3. desorden _____
4. situación _____
5. recomendar _____
6. considerar _____

B. The statements below refer to one of the roommates from the reading in your textbook. The roommates' names are Rosario and Marta. After each statement, circle **M** if it describes **Marta** or **R** if it describes **Rosario**.

1. **M R** Le gusta el orden.
2. **M R** Le gusta el desorden.
3. **M R** Su color favorito es el negro.
4. **M R** Su color favorito es el amarillo.
5. **M R** Hay comida en el suelo.
6. **M R** Hay postre en el escritorio.

C. The second part of the reading in your textbook is the response from the advice columnist, Magdalena, to Marta's letter. Read the final piece of advice below that Magdalena gives to Rosario. Answer the questions in English that follow.

> *Si la situación no es mejor después de unas semanas, tienes que considerar la posibilidad de separar el dormitorio con una cortina. ¡Pero no debe ser una cortina ni negra ni amarilla!*

1. How long does Magdalena tell Rosario to wait before considering another possibility?

   _____

2. According to Magdalena, with what should Rosario separate the room?

   _____

3. What colors should not separate the two rooms?

   _____ and _____

D. In your own words, explain what the disaster in Rosario's bedroom is.

   _____

   _____

Realidades Ⓑ

Capítulo 6A

Nombre _____

Fecha _____

Hora _____

Guided Practice Activities 6A-6

Presentación oral (p. 119)

Task: Use a photograph or drawing of a bedroom to talk about what its contents and colors tell about the personality of the owner.

A. Bring in a picture of a bedroom. It can be a photo, a picture cut out from a magazine, or a picture that you drew. Use the following four questions to organize your thoughts about the room. Write your answers to the questions on the line beneath each question.

1. ¿Qué hay en el dormitorio?

   _____

2. ¿Cómo es el dormitorio?

   _____

3. ¿De qué color es?

   _____

4. ¿Qué cosas hay en las paredes?

   _____

B. Using the information you just compiled in **part A**, answer the questions below in the spaces provided.

- En tu opinión, ¿cómo es la persona que vive (*lives*) en el dormitorio?
- ¿Qué le gusta hacer?

Es una persona _____ porque el dormitorio _____

_____.

Le gusta _____ porque en el dormitorio hay _____

_____.

C. Go through your presentation several times. Make sure you:

_____ support your statements with examples

_____ use complete sentences

_____ speak clearly

Realidades (B)

Nombre _____

Hora _____

Capítulo 6B

Fecha _____

Vocabulary Flash Cards, Sheet 1

Write the Spanish vocabulary word below each picture. If there is a word or phrase, copy it in the space provided. Be sure to include the article for each noun.

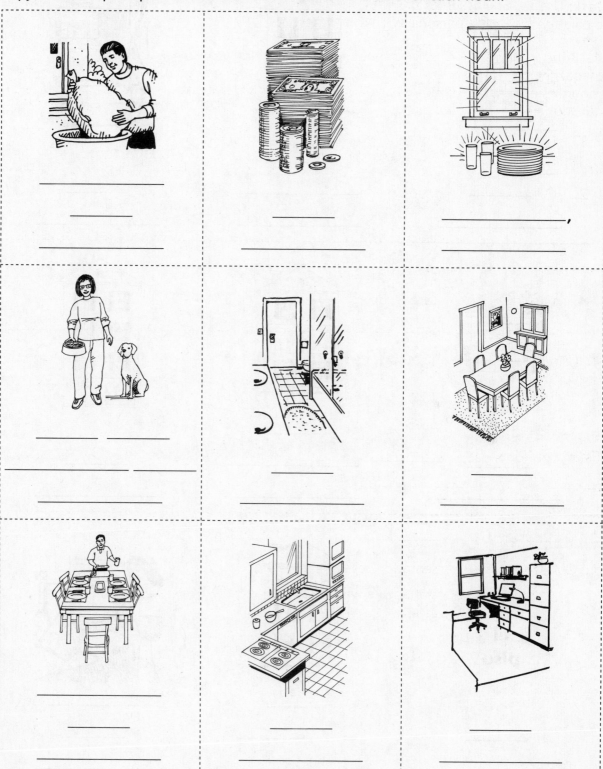

Realidades B

Capítulo 6B

Nombre _____

Hora _____

Fecha _____

Vocabulary Flash Cards, Sheet 2

_____

_____

_____

_____

_____

_____

_____

_____

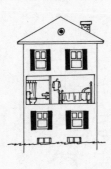

_____

_____

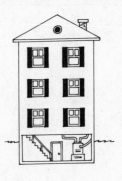

_____

_____

**el
piso**

_____

_____

_____

_____

_____

_____

_____

_____

_____

_____

_____

_____

_____

_____

_____

_____

_____

_____

_____

_____

_____

_____

_____

_____

Realidades B

Capítulo 6B

Nombre _____

Hora _____

Fecha _____

Vocabulary Flash Cards, Sheet 4

ayudar _____	cerca (de) _____ _____	los quehaceres _____
dar _____	lejos (de) _____ _____	el apartamento _____
poner _____	vivir _____	el cuarto _____ _____

Realidades **B**

Capítulo 6B

Nombre _____

Hora _____

Fecha _____

Vocabulary Flash Cards, Sheet 5

sucio, sucia

_____ ,

_____

¿Qué estás haciendo?

_____

_____

_____

si

_____

bastante

_____

un momento

_____

_____

_____

_____

¿Cuáles?

_____

_____

recibir

_____

_____

_____

sí

¿Qué
estás
haciendo?

sucio
sucia

un
momento

durante

recibir

¿Cuáles?

Tear out this page. Write the English words on the lines. Fold the paper along the dotted line to see the correct answers so you can check your work.

cerca (de)   _____

lejos (de)   _____

vivir   _____

el apartamento   _____

la cocina   _____

el comedor   _____

el despacho   _____

la escalera   _____

el garaje   _____

la planta baja   _____

el primer piso   _____

el segundo piso   _____

la sala   _____

el sótano   _____

arreglar el cuarto   _____

ayudar   _____

cocinar   _____

cortar el césped   _____

Fold In

Realidades **B**

Capítulo 6B

Nombre _____

Fecha _____

Hora _____

Vocabulary Check, Sheet 2

Tear out this page. Write the Spanish words on the lines. Fold the paper along the dotted line to see the correct answers so you can check your work.

close (to), near _____

far (from) _____

to live _____

apartment _____

kitchen _____

dining room _____

home office _____

stairs, stairway _____

garage _____

ground floor _____

second floor _____

third floor _____

living room _____

basement _____

to straighten up the room _____

to help _____

to cook _____

to cut the lawn _____

Fold In

Tear out this page. Write the English words on the lines. Fold the paper along the dotted line to see the correct answers so you can check your work.

dar de comer
al perro   _____

hacer la cama   _____

lavar los platos   _____

limpiar el baño   _____

                          _____

pasar la
aspiradora   _____

poner la mesa   _____

los quehaceres   _____

quitar el polvo   _____

sacar la basura   _____

                          _____

limpio, limpia   _____

sucio, sucia   _____

bastante   _____

el dinero   _____

recibir   _____

Fold In

Nombre _____ Hora _____

Fecha _____ **Vocabulary Check, Sheet 4**

Tear out this page. Write the Spanish words on the lines. Fold the paper along
the dotted line to see the correct answers so you can check your work.

to feed the dog   _____

                             _____

to make the bed   _____

to wash the dishes   _____

to clean the
bathroom   _____

to vacuum   _____

                             _____

to set the table   _____

chores   _____

to dust   _____

to take out
the trash   _____

clean   _____

dirty   _____

enough; rather   _____

money   _____

to receive   _____

To hear a complete list of the vocabulary for this chapter,
go to www.realidades.com and type in the Web Code jcd-0699.
Then click on **Repaso del capítulo.**

Fold In

Affirmative *tú* commands (p. 138)

- **Tú** commands are used to tell friends, family members, or peers to do something.
- **Tú** command forms are the same as the regular present-tense forms for **Ud./él/ella.**

Infinitive	*Ud./él/ella* form	Affirmative *tú* command
-ar verb: **hablar**	habla	**¡Habla!**
-er verb: **leer**	lee	**¡Lee!**
-ir verb: **escribir**	escribe	**¡Escribe!**

- Two verbs you have learned already, **hacer** and **poder**, have irregular affirmative **tú** command forms:

    poner → **pon**   **¡Pon** la mesa!

    hacer → **haz**   **¡Haz** la cama!

- You can tell the difference between a command form and an **Ud., él,** or **ella** verb form from the context of the sentence. A comma after the person's name indicates they are being talked to directly. Possessive adjectives can also help you decide if the person is being addressed directly (**tu**) or referred to in the third person (**su**).

    Marcos lee **su** libro. (**él** verb form)

    Marcos, lee **tu** libro. (command form)

A. Circle the command form in each sentence.

1. María, habla con tu hermano, por favor.
2. Tomasina, escribe tu tarea.
3. Marcos, come el almuerzo.
4. Silvia, practica la guitarra.
5. Elena, haz la cama.
6. Sandra, pon la mesa.
7. Alfonso, lee el libro.
8. Carlos, lava el coche.

B. Now look at each sentence. Write **C** if the verb is a command form. Write **no** if it is not a command form. Follow the models.

Modelos   Javier estudia en su dormitorio.   _no_

Javier, estudia en tu dormitorio.   _C_

1. Alfonso lee el libro. _____
2. Paula, ayuda a tu madre. _____
3. Roberto escucha a su madre. _____
4. Pablo hace la tarea. _____
5. Ana, lava los platos. _____
6. Isa juega con su hermana. _____
7. David, limpia la casa. _____
8. Elena, pon la mesa. _____

Realidades B

Capítulo 6B

Nombre _____

Hora _____

Fecha _____

Guided Practice Activities 6B-2

Affirmative *tú* commands *(continued)*

C. Circle the correct form of the verb to complete each sentence.

1. ¡(**Plancha** / **Planchan**) la ropa, por favor!

2. Gerardo, (**prepara** / **preparas**) la comida, por favor.

3. Alberto, (**hace** / **haz**) la tarea ahora.

4. Rosa, (**pone** / **pon**) los platos en la mesa, por favor.

5. ¡(**Lavas** / **Lava**) el coche, por favor!

6. Linda, (**juega** / **juegas**) con tu hermana esta tarde.

D. Write the affirmative **tú** command forms to complete the following conversations. Follow the model.

Modelo RAÚL: Ana, (poner) ____*pon*____ los libros en la mesa.

ANA: Sí, pero (tomar)____*toma*____ mi mochila.

1. SEBASTIÁN: Roberto, (lavar) _____ los platos, por favor.

   ROBERTO: Claro. (Traer) _____ los platos sucios aquí.

2. TERESA: Susana, (preparar) _____ el almuerzo.

   SUSANA: Sí, pero (hablar) _____ con mamá para ver qué necesitamos.

3. EDUARDO: Elena, (hacer) _____ los quehaceres.

   ELENA: Claro. (Escribir) _____ una lista.

4. ISABEL: Margarita, (planchar) _____ la ropa, por favor.

   MARGARITA: Claro, pero (sacar) _____ la plancha, por favor.

E. Write **tú** command forms to complete each sentence. Use verbs from the list.

hacer	lavar	poner	sacar

1. ¡_____ la basura!

2. ¡_____ el coche!

3. ¡_____ la mesa!

4. ¡_____ la cama!

realidades.com

• Web Code: jcd-0613

Realidades B

Capítulo 6B

Nombre _____

Hora _____

Fecha _____

Guided Practice Activities 6B-3

The present progressive tense (p. 142)

- Use the present progressive tense to say what people are doing or what is happening right now.

   Estamos lavando el coche.   *We are washing the car.*

- The present progressive tense uses forms of **estar** with the present participle.
- Review the forms of **estar**:

yo	estoy	nosotros/nosotras	estamos
tú	estás	vosotros/vosotras	estáis
usted/él/ella	está	ustedes/ellos/ellas	están

- You form the present participle for -**ar** verbs by removing the -**ar** ending and adding -**ando: preparar → preparando, hablar → hablando.**
- You form the present participle for -**er** and -**ir** verbs by removing the -**er** or -**ir** ending and adding -**iendo: comer → comiendo, escribir → escribiendo.**
- The forms of **estar** change to match the subject of the sentence. The present participle always stays the same, regardless of who the subject is.

   Francisco está limpiando la mesa.   *Francisco is cleaning the table.*

   Tú y yo estamos limpiando el baño.   *We are cleaning the bathroom.*

A. Look at each sentence. Underline the form of **estar.** Circle the present participle. Follow the model.

Modelo   Enrique está lavando los platos.

1. Tú y yo estamos pasando la aspiradora.

2. Mis abuelos están cortando el césped.

3. Mi hermana está quitando el polvo en la sala.

4. Yo estoy dando de comer al perro.

5. Ustedes están sacando la basura de la cocina.

6. Tú estás poniendo la mesa con los platos limpios.

7. Ella está haciendo las camas del segundo piso.

B. Complete each sentence with the appropriate form of **estar.**

1. Yo _____ poniendo la mesa.

2. Tú _____ sacando la basura.

3. Ella _____ lavando la ropa.

4. Nosotros _____ preparando el almuerzo.

5. Ustedes _____ cortando el césped.

The present progressive tense *(continued)*

C. Write the present participles of the verbs shown. Follow the models. Remember to use **-ando** for **-ar** verbs and **-iendo** for **-er** and **-ir** verbs.

Modelos	ayudar	*ayudando*
	hacer	*haciendo*
	escribir	*escribiendo*

1. dar _____   **5.** sacar _____

2. abrir _____   **6.** lavar _____

3. comer _____   **7.** jugar _____

4. romper _____   **8.** poner _____

D. Look at the drawing. Then write forms of the present progressive (**estar** + present participle) to complete each sentence. Follow the models.

Modelos	Graciela (dar)	*está dando*	de comer al perro.
	Lola y Elia (hablar)	*están hablando*	.

1. El padre (sacar) _____ la basura.

2. La madre (cocinar) _____ unas hamburguesas.

3. Ana María (cortar) _____ el césped.

4. Manolo y José (lavar) _____ el coche.

5. Tito y Ramón (poner) _____ la mesa.

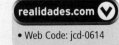

• Web Code: jcd-0614

Realidades B

Capítulo 6B

Nombre _____

Hora _____

Fecha _____

Guided Practice Activities 6B-5

Lectura: Cantaclara (pp. 146–147)

A. The reading in your textbook is similar to the story of Cinderella. Write four facts that you can remember about the Cinderella story in the spaces below. If you are not familiar with the story you will need to find out from someone who is.

1. _____

2. _____

3. _____

4. _____

B. Skim through the reading and the pictures in your textbook to find similarities between the story of Cantaclara and Cinderella. Check off any similarities in your list above.

C. Since you know that the story in your textbook is like the story of Cinderella, you know that Cantaclara lives with her stepmother and two stepsisters. Below is a dialogue with all four of them. Read the dialogue and answer the questions that follow.

> –Cantaclara, saca la basura. Y después, pon la mesa –dice la madrastra.
>
> –Cantaclara, haz mi cama y limpia el baño –dice Griselda.
>
> –Haz mi cama también –dice Hortencia.
>
> –Un momento. Estoy lavando los platos ahora mismo –dice Cantaclara.

1. Circle the names of the four people who are speaking.

2. How is a dialogue written differently in Spanish than in English?

_____

3. Which person does NOT say she wants Cantaclara to make her bed?

_____

D. Now, read what takes place at the end of the story. Answer the questions in English that follow.

> Son las ocho de la noche. La madrastra y las dos hermanastras están en la sala y ven su programa favorito. Pero, ¿qué es esto? ¡Ven a Cantaclara en la pantalla!
>
> –Mira, mamá. ¡Es Cantaclara! –dice Hortencia.
>
> –¡Oh, no! Si Cantaclara es la nueva estrella del futuro, ¿quién va a hacer los quehaceres? –pregunta Griselda.

1. At what time do the stepmother and stepsisters sit down to watch their favorite show? _____

2. Whom do they see on TV? _____

3. What problem does Griselda think of at the end? _____

Presentación escrita (p. 149)

Task: Pretend that your family is selling their house, apartment, or that you are selling an imaginary dream home. Create a flyer in Spanish to promote the sale of your home.

① Prewrite. You are going to prepare an informative flyer about your home. In order to provide the most information to potential buyers, you will need to anticipate their questions. Read the potential questions below and write answers about your home in the spaces provided.

a) En general, ¿cómo es la casa o apartamento? (¿Es grande o pequeño?)

_____.

b) ¿De qué color es la casa o apartamento?

_____.

c) ¿Cuántos cuartos hay en la casa o apartamento? ¿Cuáles son?

_____.

d) ¿Cómo son los cuartos? (¿grandes o pequeños?)

_____.

e) ¿De qué color son los cuartos?

_____.

f) ¿Cuál es la dirección (*address*) y el precio (*price*) de la casa o apartamento?

_____.

② Draft. Now, compile the answers you wrote above on a separate sheet of paper to create your rough draft. Organize your answers in a way that will be easy for anyone to read. Your flyer should also include illustrations and colored ink to make it more attractive to potential buyers. The first line on your flyer should read: **Se vende casa** (or **Se vende apartamento**).

③ Revise. Read through your ad to see that you have included all the information that a potential buyer might want. Share your draft with a partner who will check the following:

_____ Are all words spelled correctly?

_____ Is the flyer neat and attractive?

_____ Does the flyer need a visual?

_____ Is the key information provided?

_____ Does the flyer make me want to look at the property?

④ Publish. Write a new, final copy of your flyer making any necessary corrections or adding to it anything your partner suggested.

Realidades **B**

Nombre _____

Hora _____

Capítulo 7A

Fecha _____

Vocabulary Flash Cards, Sheet 1

Write the Spanish vocabulary word below each picture. If there is a word or phrase, copy it in the space provided. Be sure to include the article for each noun.

_____	_____	_____
_____	_____	_____
_____	_____	_____

_____

_____

_____

_____

_____

_____

_____

_____

_____

Realidades B

Nombre

Hora

Capítulo 7A

Fecha

Vocabulary Flash Cards, Sheet 3

buscar

_____

_____

la tienda

_____

comprar

_____

_____

la tienda de ropa

_____ _____

entrar

_____

¿En qué puedo servirle?

_____ _____

_____

_____

llevar

_____

Realidades **B**

Capítulo 7A

Nombre _____

Hora _____

Fecha _____

Vocabulary Flash Cards, Sheet 4

nuevo, nueva	Me queda(n) mal.	¡Vamos!
_____ ,	_____ _____	
_____	_____	_____
¿Cómo te queda(n)?	quizás	costar
_____		
___ _____	_____	_____
Me queda(n) bien.	Perdón.	¿Cuánto cuesta(n)...?
_____	_____	_____
_____	_____	_____

Realidades B

Capítulo 7A

Nombre _____

Fecha _____

Hora _____

Vocabulary Flash Cards, Sheet 5

el
precio

_____

_____

trescientos,
trescientas

_____,

_____

seiscientos,
seiscientas

_____,

_____

tanto

_____

cuatrocientos,
cuatrocientas

_____,

_____

setecientos,
setecientas

_____,

_____

doscientos,
doscientas

_____,

_____

quinientos,
quinientas

_____,

_____

ochocientos,
ochocientas

_____,

_____

Realidades **B**

Capítulo 7A

Nombre _____

Hora _____

Fecha _____

Vocabulary Flash Cards, Sheet 6

novecientos,
novecientas

_____ ,

_____

los
dos

_____

estos,
estas

_____ ,

_____

mil

_____

las
dos

_____

ese,
esa

_____ ,

_____

tener
razón

_____

_____

este,
esta

_____ ,

_____

esos,
esas

_____ ,

_____

Nombre _____

Hora _____

Fecha _____

Tear out this page. Write the English words on the lines. Fold the paper along the dotted line to see the correct answers so you can check your work.

buscar _____

comprar _____

el dependiente, _____
la dependienta

entrar _____

la tienda de ropa _____

el abrigo _____

la blusa _____

las botas _____

los calcetines _____

la camiseta _____

la chaqueta _____

la falda _____

la gorra _____

los jeans _____

los pantalones _____
cortos

la sudadera _____

el suéter _____

Fold In

Nombre _____

Hora _____

Fecha _____

Tear out this page. Write the Spanish words on the lines. Fold the paper along the dotted line to see the correct answers so you can check your work.

to look for _____

to buy _____

salesperson _____

_____

to enter _____

clothing store _____

coat _____

blouse _____

boots _____

socks _____

T-shirt _____

jacket _____

skirt _____

cap _____

jeans _____

shorts _____

_____

sweatshirt _____

sweater _____

Fold In

Realidades B

Nombre _____

Hora _____

Capítulo 7A

Fecha _____

Vocabulary Check, Sheet 3

Tear out this page. Write the English words on the lines. Fold the paper along the dotted line to see the correct answers so you can check your work.

el traje de baño _____

el vestido _____

los zapatos _____

llevar _____

nuevo, nueva _____

costar _____

el precio _____

doscientos _____

trescientos _____

cuatrocientos _____

quinientos _____

seiscientos _____

setecientos _____

ochocientos _____

novecientos _____

mil _____

tener razón _____

Fold In

Realidades Ⓑ

Nombre _____

Hora _____

Capítulo 7A

Fecha _____

Vocabulary Check, Sheet 4

Tear out this page. Write the Spanish words on the lines. Fold the paper along the dotted line to see the correct answers so you can check your work.

swimsuit _____

dress _____

shoes _____

to wear _____

new _____

to cost _____

price _____

two hundred _____

three hundred _____

four hundred _____

five hundred _____

six hundred _____

seven hundred _____

eight hundred _____

nine hundred _____

a thousand _____

to be correct _____

To hear a complete list of the vocabulary for this chapter, go to www.realidades.com and type in the Web Code jcd-0789. Then click on **Repaso del capítulo**.

Fold In

Stem-changing verbs: *pensar, querer,* and *preferir* (p. 168)

- Like the other stem-changing verbs you've learned (**jugar, poder,** and **dormir**), **pensar, querer,** and **preferir** use the regular present-tense endings. These endings attach to a new stem for all forms except for the **nosotros** and **vosotros** forms, which use the existing stem.

- Here are the forms of **pensar, querer,** and **preferir.** Note that in all cases, the **e** in the stem changes to **ie.**

yo	**pienso**	nosotros/nosotras	**pensamos**
tú	**piensas**	vosotros/vosotras	**pensáis**
usted/él/ella	**piensa**	ustedes/ellos/ellas	**piensan**

yo	**quiero**	nosotros/nosotras	**queremos**
tú	**quieres**	vosotros/vosotras	**queréis**
usted/él/ella	**quiere**	ustedes/ellos/ellas	**quieren**

yo	**prefiero**	nosotros/nosotras	**preferimos**
tú	**prefieres**	vosotros/vosotras	**preferís**
usted/él/ella	**prefiere**	ustedes/ellos/ellas	**prefieren**

A. Circle the forms of **pensar, querer,** or **preferir** in each sentence. Then underline the stem in each verb you circled. The first one has been done for you.

1. (Prefieren) comprar unos zapatos.

2. Queremos ir de compras.

3. Pensamos ir a la tienda de ropa.

4. ¿Prefiere Ud. el vestido o la falda?

5. Pienso comprar una sudadera.

6. ¿Quieres hablar con la dependienta?

7. Preferimos ir a una tienda grande.

8. Quieren entrar en la tienda.

B. Now, write the forms of **pensar, querer,** and **preferir** that you circled in **part A** next to each subject pronoun.

1. ellos (preferir) _____

2. nosotros (querer) _____

3. nosotros (pensar) _____

4. Ud. (preferir) _____

5. yo (pensar) _____

6. tú (querer) _____

7. nosotros (preferir) _____

8. ellos (querer) _____

Realidades B

Nombre _____

Hora _____

Capítulo 7A

Fecha _____

Guided Practice Activities 7A-2

Stem-changing verbs *(continued)*

C. Circle the correct form of **pensar**, **querer**, or **preferir** to complete each sentence.

1. Yo (**quiere / quiero**) comprar unas botas nuevas.

2. Ella (**prefiere / prefieren**) los pantalones cortos a la falda.

3. Nosotros (**prefieren / preferimos**) ir de compras en una tienda grande.

4. Ellos (**pienso / piensan**) comprar dos abrigos nuevos.

5. Tú y yo (**pensamos / piensas**) buscar una tienda con precios buenos.

6. Ustedes (**quieres / quieren**) hablar con la dependienta.

7. Nosotros (**queremos / quieres**) entrar en la tienda de ropa.

8. Tú y yo no (**piensan / pensamos**) comprar ropa hoy.

D. Complete the sentences with forms of **pensar**, **querer**, or **preferir**. Follow the models.

Modelos Tú (**pensar**) comprar un suéter.

Tú _____*piensas*_____ comprar un suéter.

Tú y yo (**preferir**) comprar el vestido azul.

Tú y yo _____*preferimos*_____ comprar el vestido azul.

1. Elena (**pensar**) comprar una sudadera.

   Elena _____ comprar una sudadera.

2. Sandra y yo (**querer**) ir a una tienda de ropa grande.

   Sandra y yo _____ ir a una tienda de ropa grande.

3. Yo (**preferir**) hablar con un dependiente.

   Yo _____ hablar con un dependiente.

4. Nosotras (**pensar**) que es un precio bueno.

   Nosotras _____ que es un precio bueno.

5. Tú (**querer**) entrar en una tienda de ropa grande.

   Tú _____ entrar en una tienda de ropa grande.

6. Tú y yo (**querer**) comprar unas camisetas nuevas.

   Tú y yo _____ comprar unas camisetas nuevas.

7. Tomás y Sebastián (**preferir**) no comprar ropa hoy.

   Tomás y Sebastián _____ no comprar ropa hoy.

8. Yo (**pensar**) comprar una gorra y un suéter.

   Yo _____ comprar una gorra y un suéter.

realidades.com

• Web Code: jcd-0704

Demonstrative adjectives (p. 172)

- Demonstrative adjectives are the equivalent of **this, that, these,** and **those** in English. You use them to point out nouns: **this hat, those shoes**.
- In Spanish, the demonstrative adjectives agree with the noun they accompany in both gender and number.

	Close		Farther away	
Singular masculine	**este** suéter	(*this* sweater)	**ese** suéter	(*that* sweater)
Singular feminine	**esta** falda	(*this* skirt)	**esa** falda	(*that* skirt)
Plural masculine	**estos** suéteres	(*these* sweaters)	**esos** suéteres	(*those* sweaters)
Plural feminine	**estas** faldas	(*these* skirts)	**esas** faldas	(*those* skirts)

A. Circle the demonstrative adjective in each sentence below. Write **C** next to the sentence if the object referred to is *close* (**este, esta, estos, estas**). Write **F** if the object referred to is *farther away* (**ese, esa, esos, esas**).

1. Me gustan estos zapatos. _____
2. Quiero comprar esas camisetas. _____
3. ¿Prefieres esta falda? _____
4. Esa camisa es muy bonita. _____
5. No me gustan esos vestidos. _____
6. ¿Te gustan estas chaquetas? _____

B. Circle the correct demonstrative adjective in each sentence.

1. ¿Cómo me quedan (**esto** / **estos**) pantalones?
2. Me gustan (**esas** / **esos**) sudaderas.
3. ¿Prefieres (**esta** / **este**) chaqueta?
4. Pienso comprar (**estos** / **este**) calcetines.
5. No me gusta (**ese** / **esa**) abrigo.
6. ¿Cómo me queda (**este** / **esta**) traje?
7. (**Eso** / **Esas**) botas son muy bonitas.
8. ¿Vas a comprar (**esos** / **esas**) pantalones cortos?

Realidades B

Capítulo 7A

Nombre _____

Hora _____

Fecha _____

Guided Practice Activities 7A-4

Demonstrative adjectives *(continued)*

C. Choose the correct form of the demonstrative adjective and write it next to each noun. Follow the models.

Close: este, esta, estos, estas   Farther: ese, esa, esos, esas

Modelos	calcetines (close): _____*estos*_____ calcetines
	camisa (farther): _____*esa*_____ camisa

1. abrigo (farther): _____ abrigo

2. botas (farther): _____ botas

3. jeans (close): _____ jeans

4. falda (close): _____ falda

5. traje de baño (close): _____ traje de baño

6. zapatos (farther): _____ zapatos

7. chaquetas (farther): _____ chaquetas

8. pantalones (close): _____ pantalones

9. vestido (farther): _____ vestido

10. suéter (close): _____ suéter

D. In each drawing below, the item of clothing that is larger is closer to you. The one that is smaller is farther away. Write the correct demonstrative adjective to indicate the item that is marked with an arrow. Follow the model.

Modelo	 _____*esta*_____ camisa

1.  _____ pantalones

2.  _____ sudaderas

3.  _____ vestido

4.  _____ zapatos

5.  _____ abrigo

realidades.com
• Web Code: jcd-0703

Lectura: Tradiciones de la ropa panameña (pp. 176–177)

A. You will find out a lot about the contents of the reading in your textbook by looking at the title and the photos. In the spaces below, write three main topics that you would expect a reading on Panamanian culture to cover.

1. _____

2. _____

3. _____

B. Read the paragraph below on **polleras** and answer the questions that follow in Spanish.

> *Una tradición panameña de mucho orgullo (pride) es llevar el vestido típico de las mujeres, "la pollera". Hay dos tipos de pollera, la pollera montuna y la pollera de gala, que se lleva en los festivales.*

1. Según la lectura, ¿cómo se llama el vestido típico de las mujeres en Panamá?

_____

2. ¿Cuáles son los dos tipos de pollera?

_____ y _____

3. ¿Cuándo se lleva la pollera de gala? _____

C. Look through the reading in your textbook again to find whether the following statements are true or false. Then, circle **cierto** for true or **falso** for false.

1. cierto falso Hay un Día Nacional de la Pollera en la ciudad de Las Tablas.

2. cierto falso Las Tablas es famosa por ser el mejor lugar para celebrar los carnavales.

3. cierto falso El canal de Panamá conecta el océano Pacífico con el lago Titicaca.

4. cierto falso Panamá es un istmo.

5. cierto falso El segundo tipo de ropa auténtico de Panamá que se menciona es la gorra de Panamá.

Presentación oral (p. 179)

Task: You and a partner will play the roles of a customer and a salesclerk. The customer will look at various items in the store, talk with the clerk, and then decide if he or she would like to buy anything.

A. Work with a partner to prepare the skit. You will be the customer. You and your partner will need to discuss what type of clothing your store is selling. You will then need a name for your store and some samples of merchandise to use in your skit. You may bring in clothes or use cutouts from a magazine. Complete the following in the spaces below:

Type of clothing: _____

Store name: _____

B. Now, make a list below of five different expressions and questions that will help you play your role. You may want to look back in the *A primera vista* and *Videohistoria* sections in your textbook for ideas to help you get started.

1. _____
2. _____
3. _____
4. _____
5. _____

C. Work with your partner to put together and practice your presentation. Keep in mind the following things:

_____ to answer questions using complete sentences

_____ to speak clearly

_____ to keep the conversation going

_____ to finish the conversation at a logical point

D. When you present your skit, the clerk will begin the conversation. That means that you will need to respond as your first action. As your last action, you will need to decide whether or not to buy something. Your teacher will grade you based on the following:

- how well you keep the conversation going
- how complete your presentation is
- how well you use new and previously learned vocabulary

Write the Spanish vocabulary word below each picture. If there is a word or phrase, copy it in the space provided. Be sure to include the article for each noun.

Realidades **B**

Capítulo 7B

Nombre _____

Fecha _____

Hora _____

Vocabulary Flash Cards, Sheet 2

_____

_____

_____

_____

**en la
Red**

_____

_____

_____

_____

_____

_____

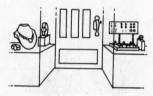

_____

_____

_____

_____

_____

_____

_____

_____

Realidades B

Capítulo 7B

Nombre _____

Fecha _____

Hora _____

Vocabulary Flash Cards, Sheet 3

**el
novio**

_____

**caro,
cara**

_____,

**la
novia**

_____

mirar

_____

**barato,
barata**

_____,

_____

**pagar
(por)**

_____

Realidades B

Capítulo 7B

Nombre

Hora

Fecha

Vocabulary Flash Cards, Sheet 4

vender

_____

ayer

_____

**hace
+ _time
expression_**

_____

_____

_____

anoche

_____

**la semana
pasada**

_____ _____

_____

_____

_____

**el año
pasado**

_____

_____

¡Uf!

_____

_____

Realidades B

Nombre _____

Hora _____

Capítulo 7B

Fecha _____

Vocabulary Check, Sheet 1

Tear out this page. Write the English words on the lines. Fold the paper along the dotted line to see the correct answers so you can check your work.

el almacén _____

_____

en la Red _____

la joyería _____

la librería _____

la tienda de
descuentos _____

la tienda de
electrodomésticos _____

la zapatería _____

el anillo _____

los anteojos de sol _____

los aretes _____

el bolso _____

la cadena _____

la cartera _____

el collar _____

la corbata _____

los guantes _____

el llavero _____

Fold In →

Realidades B

Capítulo 7B

Nombre _____

Hora _____

Fecha _____

Vocabulary Check, Sheet 2

Tear out this page. Write the Spanish words on the lines. Fold the paper along the dotted line to see the correct answers so you can check your work.

department
store   _____

online   _____

jewelry store   _____

bookstore   _____

discount store   _____

                         _____

household
appliance store   _____

                         _____

shoe store   _____

ring   _____

sunglasses   _____

earrings   _____

purse   _____

chain   _____

wallet   _____

necklace   _____

tie   _____

gloves   _____

key chain   _____

Fold In

Nombre _____ Hora _____

Fecha _____ **Vocabulary Check, Sheet 3**

Tear out this page. Write the English words on the lines. Fold the paper along the dotted line to see the correct answers so you can check your work.

el perfume _____

la pulsera _____

el reloj pulsera _____

el software _____

el novio _____

la novia _____

barato,
barata _____

caro, cara _____

mirar _____

pagar (por) _____

vender _____

Fold In

Tear out this page. Write the Spanish words on the lines. Fold the paper along the dotted line to see the correct answers so you can check your work.

perfume   _____

bracelet   _____

watch   _____

software   _____

boyfriend   _____

girlfriend   _____

inexpensive,   _____
cheap

expensive   _____

to look (at)   _____

to pay (for)   _____

to sell   _____

Fold In

To hear a complete list of the vocabulary for this chapter, go to www.realidades.com and type in the Web Code jcd-0799. Then click on **Repaso del capítulo.**

The preterite of *-ar* verbs (p. 196)

- The preterite is a Spanish past tense that is used to talk about actions that were completed in the past: *I went to the store. I bought a jacket.*
- To form the preterite of **-ar** verbs, you take the stem of the verb (the same stem you used to form the present tense) and add the following endings:

hablar → habl- + endings

yo	habl**é**	nosotros/nosotras	habl**amos**
tú	habl**aste**	vosotros/vosotras	habl**asteis**
usted/él/ella	habl**ó**	ustedes/ellos/ellas	habl**aron**

- Notice the accents on the **yo** and **usted/él/ella** forms: habl**é**, habl**ó**.

A. Underline the preterite verb forms in the following conversations. **¡Ojo!** Not all the verb forms are preterite forms.

1. ELENA:　¿Hablaste con Enrique ayer?

   ANA:　Sí, hablamos por teléfono anoche. Él trabajó ayer.

   ELENA:　¿Ah, sí? ¿Dónde trabaja?

   ANA:　Trabaja en un restaurante. Ayer lavó muchos platos y limpió las mesas.

2. MARCOS:　¿Estudiaste para el examen?

   TOMÁS:　Sí, estudié mucho, pero estoy nervioso.

   MARCOS:　Yo también. Pasé dos horas en la biblioteca.

   TOMÁS:　Yo estudié en casa y usé la computadora.

B. Now, fill in the conversations from **part A** with the missing preterite forms.

1. ELENA:　¿_____ con Enrique ayer?

   ANA:　Sí, _____ por teléfono anoche. Él _____ ayer.

   ELENA:　¿Ah, sí? ¿Dónde trabaja?

   ANA:　Trabaja en un restaurante. Ayer _____ muchos platos y _____ las mesas.

2. MARCOS:　¿_____ para el examen?

   TOMÁS:　Sí, _____ mucho, pero estoy nervioso.

   MARCOS:　Yo también. _____ dos horas en la biblioteca.

   TOMÁS:　Yo _____ en casa y _____ la computadora.

realidades.com
- Web Code: jbd-0713

Realidades B

Capítulo 7B

Nombre _____

Fecha _____

Hora _____

Guided Practice Activities 7B-2

The preterite of -*ar* verbs *(continued)*

C. Circle the correct preterite form to complete each sentence.

1. Yo (**caminó** / **caminé**) por dos horas ayer.

2. Ellos (**hablaste** / **hablaron**) por teléfono anoche.

3. Nosotros (**cocinamos** / **cocinaron**) la cena.

4. Tú (**cantaron** / **cantaste**) en la ópera.

5. Ella (**escuchó** / **escucharon**) música en su dormitorio.

6. Ustedes (**levantaron** / **levantamos**) pesas en el gimnasio.

D. Write the missing preterite forms in the chart.

	cantar	bailar	escuchar	lavar	nadar
yo	canté				
tú		bailaste			
Ud./él/ella			escuchó		
nosotros/nosotras				lavamos	
Uds./ellos/ellas					nadaron

E. Write the correct preterite form of the verb indicated next to each subject pronoun. Follow the model.

Modelo   tú (bailar) _____*bailaste*_____

1. yo (cantar) _____

2. ella (nadar) _____

3. Ud. (esquiar) _____

4. ellos (lavar) _____

5. nosotros (dibujar) _____

6. ellos (pasar) _____

7. tú (hablar) _____

8. yo (limpiar) _____

F. Use verbs from the list to say what you and your friends did last night.

estudiar   trabajar   hablar por teléfono   bailar   cantar   cocinar escuchar música   esquiar   lavar la ropa   levantar pesas   limpiar el baño

1. Anoche yo _____.

2. Yo no _____.

3. Anoche mis amigos _____.

4. Nosotros no _____.

realidades.com

• Web Code: jcd-0713

Capítulo 7B   Fecha _____   **Guided Practice Activities 7B-3**

The preterite of verbs ending in *-car* and *-gar* (p. 198)

- Verbs that end in **-car** and **-gar** use the same preterite endings as regular **-ar** verbs, except in the **yo** form.
- Here are the preterite forms of **buscar** (*to look for*) and **pagar** (*to pay*).

c → qu

yo	**busqué**	nosotros/nosotras	**buscamos**
tú	**buscaste**	vosotros/vosotras	**buscasteis**
usted/él/ella	**buscó**	ustedes/ellos/ellas	**buscaron**

g → gu

yo	**pagué**	nosotros/nosotras	**pagamos**
tú	**pagaste**	vosotros/vosotras	**pagasteis**
usted/él/ella	**pagó**	ustedes/ellos/ellas	**pagaron**

- Other verbs you know follow this pattern. **Jugar** is like **pagar (g → gu)**. **Practicar**, **sacar**, and **tocar** are like **buscar (c → qu)**.

A. Fill in the missing **yo** forms in the chart.

	buscar	pagar	jugar	practicar	sacar	tocar
yo						
tú	buscaste	pagaste	jugaste	practicaste	sacaste	tocaste
Ud./él/ella	buscó	pagó	jugó	practicó	sacó	tocó
nosotros/nosotras	buscamos	pagamos	jugamos	practicamos	sacamos	tocamos
Uds./ellos/ellas	buscaron	pagaron	jugaron	practicaron	sacaron	tocaron

B. Write the correct forms of the verb indicated next to each subject pronoun. Follow the model.

Modelo   (pagar): tú _____*pagaste*_____

1. (pagar): ellos _____
2. (pagar): yo _____
3. (pagar): él _____
4. (jugar): tú y yo _____
5. (jugar): yo _____
6. (jugar): Uds. _____
7. (buscar): ellos _____
8. (buscar): yo _____
9. (practicar): yo _____
10. (practicar): tú _____
11. (sacar): Ud. _____
12. (sacar): yo _____
13. (tocar): yo _____
14. (tocar): tú y yo _____

realidades.com Ⓥ
• Web Code: jcd-0714

Realidades B

Capítulo 7B

Nombre _____

Hora _____

Fecha _____

Guided Practice Activities 7B-4

Direct object pronouns (p. 202)

- A direct object tells who or what receives the action of the verb:

  Busco una <u>cadena</u>.   *I am looking for a <u>chain</u>.*

- In the sentence above, **cadena** is the direct object noun.

- You can use a direct object pronoun to replace a direct object noun.

- The direct object pronoun must match the noun it replaces in both gender and number:

  Compré <u>un suéter</u>.   → **Lo** compré. (*masculine, singular*)

  Compré <u>una falda</u>.   → **La** compré. (*feminine singular*)

  Compré <u>unos aretes</u>.   → **Los** compré. (*masculine plural*)

  Compré <u>unas pulseras</u>.   → **Las** compré. (*feminine plural*)

- The direct object comes *before* a verb in the present tense or the preterite tense.

  Lo tengo aquí. (*I have **it** here.*)

  Lo compré anoche. (*I bought **it** last night.*)

A. Underline the direct object noun in each sentence.

1. Busco unos guantes nuevos.
2. La dependienta vendió el perfume.
3. Compré dos llaveros.
4. Llevamos nuestras carteras.
5. Compramos un collar.
6. Miramos unas corbatas.
7. Buscaron una cadena.
8. Preparé el almuerzo.

B. Write each noun you circled in **part A** on the following lines. Write **M** or **F** next to the noun, depending on whether it is masculine or feminine. Then write **S** or **P** next to that, depending on whether the noun is singular or plural. Follow the model.

Modelo   _____*guantes*_____   _M, P_

1. _____ _____
2. _____ _____
3. _____ _____
4. _____ _____

5. _____ _____
6. _____ _____
7. _____ _____

C. Now, write the correct direct object pronoun to replace each noun you wrote in **part B**. Follow the model.

Modelo   guantes, M, P: _____*Los*_____ busqué.

1. _____ vendió.
2. _____ compré.
3. _____ llevamos.
4. _____ compramos.

5. _____ miramos.
6. _____ buscaron.
7. _____ preparé.

realidades.com

• Web Code: jcd-0715

Realidades **B**

Capítulo 7B

Nombre _____

Fecha _____

Hora _____

Guided Practice Activities 7B-5

Lectura: ¡De compras! (pp. 208–209)

A. The reading in your textbook is about shopping in Hispanic communities of four different U.S. cities: New York, Miami, Los Angeles, and San Antonio. Use what you know about each area of the country and make a list of three items you would expect to find in Hispanic shopping centers in each city.

1. New York

a) _____

b) _____

c) _____

2. Miami

a) _____

b) _____

c) _____

3. Los Angeles

a) _____

b) _____

c) _____

4. San Antonio

a) _____

b) _____

c) _____

B. Now, look at the descriptions from the reading in your textbook and decide which city is being described. Write the name of the city in the space provided. Each city will be used once.

1. _____ Hay bodegas que venden productos típicos cubanos.

2. _____ En las joyerías de la calle Olvera, venden joyas de plata: aretes, collares, anillos y mucho más.

3. _____ En la calle 116, venden ropa, comida típica del Caribe, discos compactos, libros y mucho más.

4. _____ Es esta ciudad bonita, hay tiendas de artesanías mexicanas que son fabulosas.

C. The narrator from the reading in your textbook buys things in each city. Some items may have been on your list in **part A**. Look at the things below that the narrator bought. Write the name of the city for each in the spaces provided.

1. _____ una piñata

2. _____ una camiseta con la bandera de Puerto Rico

3. _____ pasta de guayaba

4. _____ un sarape

5. _____ una pulsera bonita

6. _____ una blusa bordada

Presentación escrita (p. 211)

Task: Write a letter to a cousin or other relative about a gift you bought for a member of your family. Let the relative know what you bought so that he or she will not buy the same item.

❶ Prewrite. Think of a birthday gift you bought for a family member's birthday. It could be current or in the past. Answer the following questions about the gift to help organize your thoughts. Use complete sentences when you answer.

1. ¿Para quién es el regalo? _____

2. ¿Qué compraste? _____

3. ¿Dónde compraste el regalo? _____

4. ¿Por qué compraste ese regalo? _____

5. ¿Cuánto pagaste por el regalo? _____

❷ Draft. Use the form below to write a rough draft of your letter. Include all of the information you wrote in your answers in **part 1**. Look in your textbook for a model to help you.

Querido(a) _____:
            (*name of the relative you are writing to*)

Compré _____ para _____.

Lo compré en _____.

Creo que _____.

Pagué _____.

Tu _____,
    (*your relationship to the person*)

_____
        (*your name*)

❸ Revise. Read your letter again before you give it to a partner to review. Your teacher will check:

- how easy the letter is to understand
- how much information is included about the gift
- how appropriate the greeting and closing are
- the accuracy of the use of the preterite

Write the Spanish vocabulary word below each picture. If there is a word or phrase, copy it in the space provided. Be sure to include the article for each noun.

la ciudad _____	**el mar** _____	**el país** _____
   _____	 _____	 _____
 _____ _____	 _____ _____	 _____ _____

_____

_____

el
animal

_____

_____

_____

_____

_____

el
árbol

_____

_____

el
oso

_____

_____

_____

_____

la
atracción

_____

_____

_____

_____

aprender (a)

_____ ___

_____

tomar
el sol

_____

bucear

_____

montar a
caballo

_____ ___

visitar

_____

comprar
recuerdos

_____

_____ ___

el
lugar

_____

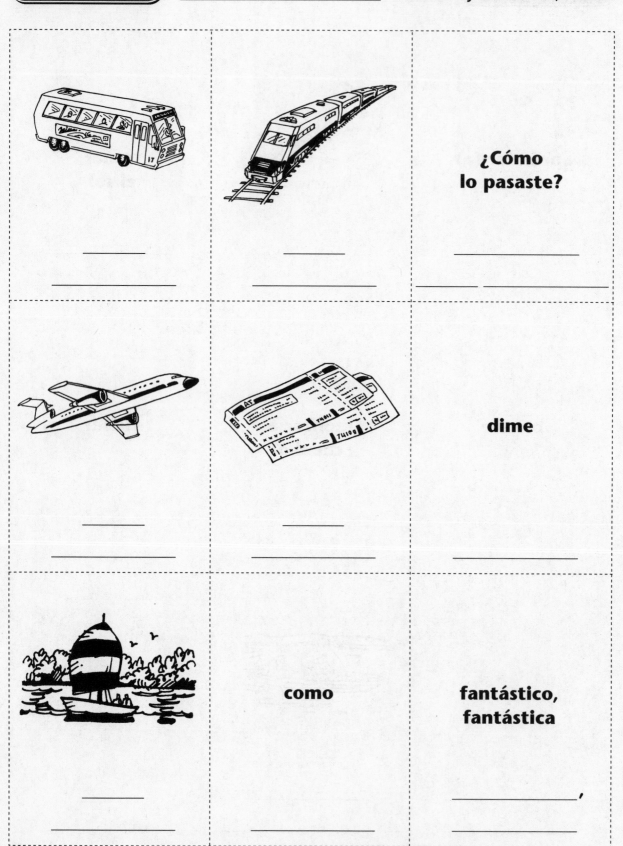

¿Cómo lo pasaste?

_____

_____

dime

_____

como

fantástico, fantástica

_____

Fue un desastre.	**ir de vacaciones**	**¿Qué te pasó?**
___ ___ _____	_____	_____ ___ ___
el hotel	**Me gustó.**	**regresar**
___ _____	___ _____	_____
impresionante	**¿Qué hiciste?**	**salir**
_____	_____	_____

Realidades **B**

Capítulo 8A

Nombre _____

Hora _____

Fecha _____

Vocabulary Flash Cards, Sheet 6

¿Te gustó?

_____

_____

¿Viste...?

_____

durante

_____

tremendo, tremenda

_____ ,

_____

viajar

_____

tarde

_____

vi

_____

el viaje

_____

_____

temprano

_____

Tear out this page. Write the English words on the lines. Fold the paper along the dotted line to see the correct answers so you can check your work.

la ciudad   _____

el estadio   _____

el lago   _____

el mar   _____

el monumento   _____

el museo   _____

el país   _____

el parque de
diversiones   _____
                             _____

el parque
nacional   _____

la obra de
teatro   _____

el zoológico   _____

el árbol   _____

el mono   _____

el oso   _____

el pájaro   _____

aprender (a)   _____

Fold In

Realidades **B**

Nombre _____

Hora _____

Capítulo 8A

Fecha _____

Vocabulary Check, Sheet 2

Tear out this page. Write the Spanish words on the lines. Fold the paper along the dotted line to see the correct answers so you can check your work.

city _____

stadium _____

lake _____

sea _____

monument _____

museum _____

country _____

amusement
park _____

national park _____

_____

play _____

_____

zoo _____

tree _____

monkey _____

bear _____

bird _____

to learn _____

Fold In

Tear out this page. Write the English words on the lines. Fold the paper along the dotted line to see the correct answers so you can check your work.

bucear   _____
                    _____

recuerdos   _____

descansar   _____

montar a   _____
caballo   _____

pasear en bote   _____

tomar el sol   _____

el autobús   _____

el avión   _____

el barco   _____

el tren   _____

ir de   _____
vacaciones   _____

regresar   _____

salir   _____
                    _____

viajar   _____

el viaje   _____

Fold In →

Realidades Ⓑ

Capítulo 8A

Nombre

Fecha

Hora

Vocabulary Check, Sheet 4

Tear out this page. Write the Spanish words on the lines. Fold the paper along the dotted line to see the correct answers so you can check your work.

to scuba dive/
snorkel _____

souvenirs _____

to rest, to relax _____

to ride
horseback _____
_____

to go boating _____

to sunbathe _____

bus _____

airplane _____

boat, ship _____

train _____

to go on
vacation _____
_____

to return _____

to leave,
to get out _____

to travel _____

trip _____

To hear a complete list of the vocabulary for this chapter, go to www.realidades.com and type in the Web Code jcd-0889. Then click on **Repaso del capítulo**.

Fold In

Realidades B

Nombre _____

Hora _____

Capítulo 8A

Fecha _____

Guided Practice Activities 8A-1

The preterite of *-er* and *-ir* verbs (p. 230)

- Regular **-er** and **-ir** verbs have their own set of preterite (past-tense) endings, just as they do in the present tense.
- The preterite endings for regular **-er** and **-ir** verbs are exactly the same.

comer → com- + endings			
yo	**comí**	nosotros/nosotras	**comimos**
tú	**comiste**	vosotros/vosotras	**comisteis**
usted/él/ella	**comió**	ustedes/ellos/ellas	**comieron**

escribir → escrib- + endings			
yo	**escribí**	nosotros/nosotras	**escribimos**
tú	**escribiste**	vosotros/vosotras	**escribisteis**
usted/él/ella	**escribió**	ustedes/ellos/ellas	**escribieron**

- Like regular **-ar** verbs in the preterite, regular **-er** and **-ir** verbs have an accent at the end of the **yo** and **usted/él/ella** forms: **comí**, **escribió**.

A. Write the missing preterite forms in the chart.

	comer	escribir	aprender	salir	correr
yo	comí				
tú		escribiste			
Ud./él/ella			aprendió		
nosotros/nosotras				salimos	
Uds./ellos/ellas					corrieron

B. Circle the correct preterite form to complete each sentence.

1. Sofía (**comí** / **comió**) en un restaurante mexicano.

2. Ellos (**escribimos** / **escribieron**) una tarjeta a sus abuelos.

3. Tú (**aprendiste** / **aprendió**) a hablar español.

4. Yo (**salí** / **saliste**) para el trabajo.

5. Tú y yo (**corrieron** / **corrimos**) en el parque anoche.

6. Marta y Marcos (**comió** / **comieron**) el almuerzo en la cafetería.

7. Yo (**aprendí** / **aprendió**) a montar en monopatín.

8. Usted (**salió** / **salieron**) después de las clases.

- Web Code: jcd-0803

Realidades Ⓑ

Capítulo 8A

Nombre _____

Fecha _____

Hora _____

Guided Practice Activities 8A-2

The preterite of -er and -ir verbs (continued)

C. Complete the following sentences with the correct form of the verb in parentheses. Follow the model.

Modelo   Tú (comer) _____comiste_____ en la cafetería.

1. Nosotros (escribir) _____ unas tarjetas.

2. Tú (aprender) _____ a esquiar.

3. Yo (correr) _____ en el parque.

4. Ellos (salir) _____ de la escuela a las tres.

5. Ud. (comer) _____ una hamburguesa.

6. Nosotros (ver) _____ un video anoche.

7. Ustedes (compartir) _____ una pizza.

8. Tú y yo (aprender) _____ a montar en monopatín.

9. Yo (vivir) _____ en un apartamento.

10. Ella (comprender) _____ la lección de ayer.

D. Use verbs from the list to say what you and your friends did last week.

aprender a ver	comer salir de	compartir salir con	escribir correr

1. Yo no _____ .

2. Yo no _____ .

3. Mis amigos y yo _____ .

4. Mis amigos y yo no _____ .

• Web Code: jcd-0803

The preterite of *ir* (p. 232)

- **Ir** (*to go*) is an irregular verb in the present tense. It is also irregular in the preterite tense. Here are the preterite forms of **ir**.

yo	**fui**	nosotros/nosotras	**fuimos**
tú	**fuiste**	vosotros/vosotras	**fuisteis**
usted/él/ella	**fue**	ustedes/ellos/ellas	**fueron**

- The preterite forms of **ir** are the same as the preterite forms of the verb **ser** (*to be*). You can tell which verb is meant by the meaning of the sentence.

  Marcos **fue** a Nueva York. *Marcos **went** to New York.*

  Fue un viaje fabuloso. ***It was** a fabulous trip.*

A. Add the correct ending onto the preterite stem of **ir** to create its complete preterite form. Then rewrite the complete form. Follow the model.

Modelo yo fu*i*___ _____*fui*_____

1. yo fu_____ _____
2. tú fu_____ _____
3. ella fu_____ _____
4. nosotros fu_____ _____
5. ellos fu_____ _____
6. ustedes fu_____ _____

B. Circle the correct form of **ir** to complete each sentence.

1. Yo (**fue** / **fui**) a la tienda de ropa.
2. Ellos (**fueron** / **fuiste**) al estadio de béisbol.
3. Tú (**fueron** / **fuiste**) a un parque nacional.
4. Nosotros (**fuimos** / **fueron**) al parque de diversiones.
5. Ud. (**fui** / **fue**) al teatro.
6. Uds. (**fuiste** / **fueron**) a la ciudad para comprar ropa.
7. Tú y yo (**fuimos** / **fuiste**) al mar para bucear.

C. Complete each sentence by writing in the correct form of **ir**.

1. Yo _____ a un lugar muy bonito.
2. Tú _____ al estadio de fútbol americano.
3. Ella _____ al lago para pasear en bote.
4. Nosotros _____ a la playa para tomar el sol.
5. Ellos _____ al teatro para ver una obra de teatro.
6. Ud. _____ al monumento en el parque nacional.

Realidades Ⓑ

Capítulo 8A

Nombre _____

Fecha _____

Hora _____

Guided Practice Activities 8A-4

The personal *a* (p. 236)

- You have learned to identify the direct object of a sentence. The direct object tells who or what receives the action of the verb.

  Compré <u>un anillo</u>.   *I bought <u>a ring</u>.*

  Vi <u>una obra de teatro</u>.   *I saw <u>a play</u>.*

- When the direct object is a person, a group of people, or a pet, you use **a** in front of the direct object. This use of the personal **a** has no equivalent in English and is not translated.

  Vi <u>un video</u>.   *I saw <u>a video</u>.*

  Vi **a mi abuela**.   *I saw <u>my grandmother</u>.*

  Vi **a mi perro León**.   *I saw <u>my dog León</u>.*

A. Underline the direct object in each sentence.

1. Vi un video.
2. Escribo una carta.
3. Visitaron a su familia.
4. Comimos una pizza.
5. Compraste una corbata.
6. Buscamos a nuestro perro.

B. Now, go look at each sentence from **part A** and write **P** next to those that refer to people or pets.

1. Vi un video. _____
2. Escribo una carta. _____
3. Visitaron a su familia. _____
4. Comimos una pizza. _____
5. Compraste una corbata. _____
6. Buscamos a nuestro perro. _____

C. Look at the sentences above in **part B** that you labeled with a **P**. Circle the personal **a** in each of those sentences.

D. Look at each sentence. If it requires a personal **a**, circle the **a** in parentheses. If it does not require a personal **a**, cross out the **a** in parentheses.

1. Compramos (a) un traje de baño y unos anteojos de sol.
2. Yo vi (a) un monumento grande en el parque nacional.
3. Escribimos muchas tarjetas (a) nuestros primos.
4. Visité (a) mi familia durante las vacaciones.
5. Lavaron (a) su perro Fifí.
6. Buscamos (a) una tienda de ropa buena.
7. Compré (a) un boleto de avión ayer.
8. Busqué (a) mi hermano menor en el parque de atracciones.

realidades.com Ⓥ
- Web Code: jcd-0805

Realidades B

Capítulo 8A

Nombre _____

Fecha _____

Hora _____

Guided Practice Activities 8A-5

Lectura: Álbum de mi viaje a Perú (pp. 240–241)

A. Sometimes you can use clues from the context of what you are reading to help discover the meaning of the word. Try to find the meaning of the five words listed below by using context clues from the reading in your textbook. Write in the English equivalent of each word in the space provided.

1. antigua _____

2. impresionantes _____

3. altura _____

4. construyeron _____

5. nivel _____

B. The reading in your textbook is a journal entry from a trip to Perú by the author Sofía Porrúa. Each day that she writes in the journal, she is in a different location. Choose the location from the word bank and write it next to the day to which it corresponds.

Cuzco	Machu Picchu	sobre las líneas de Nazca	en el lago Titicaca	Lima

1. domingo, 25 de julio _____

2. miércoles, 28 de julio _____

3. jueves, 29 de julio _____

4. sábado, 31 de julio _____

5. miércoles, 4 de agosto _____

C. In the first log entry, Sofía mentions her two companions, Beto and Carmen. Read the passage below about these two friends and answer the questions that follow.

> *Beto está sacando muchas fotos con su cámara digital. Carmen está dibujando todo lo que ve. Las montañas son fantásticas.*

1. Sofía is capturing the trip by keeping a journal. How is Beto capturing the trip?
_____ And Carmen? _____

2. What is Beto using to capture the trip? _____

   What do you think Carmen is using? _____

Realidades Ⓑ

Capítulo 8A

Nombre _____

Fecha _____

Hora _____

Guided Practice Activities 8A-6

Presentación oral (p. 243)

Task: You will talk about a trip you took. It can be a real or an imaginary trip. Use photographs or drawings to make your talk more interesting.

A. Think about the specifics of your trip. Answer the questions below in Spanish with as much detail as you can think of. Use complete sentences.

1. ¿Cuándo fuiste de viaje? _____

   _____

2. ¿Qué hiciste en tu viaje? _____

   _____

3. ¿Qué lugares visitaste? _____

   _____

4. ¿A quiénes viste? _____

   _____

5. ¿Compraste algo? _____ ¿Qué compraste? _____

   _____

B. You will need to create a visual presentation to go along with your talk. You can bring in actual photos or you can create drawings of a trip. Organize and attach your drawings or photos to a piece of posterboard. A good way to do this would be to put them in order of when they happened, going from the top to the bottom of the page.

C. Read the following model before you write up the script for your talk. Notice that you should add how you felt about the trip at the end.

> *En marzo de este año, fui a Florida para visitar a mi abuelita y a mis primos. Tomamos el sol en la playa y nadamos mucho. Aprendí a bucear y vi animales muy interesantes en el mar. Me gusta mucho Florida. Es un lugar fantástico. El viaje fue muy divertido.*

D. Now, write what you are going to say about your trip on the lines below. Remember to refer back to your photos or drawings.

_____

_____

_____

_____

Realidades B

Capítulo 8B

Nombre _____

Fecha _____

Hora _____

Vocabulary Flash Cards, Sheet 1

Write the Spanish vocabulary word below each picture. If there is a word or phrase, copy it in the space provided. Be sure to include the article for each noun.

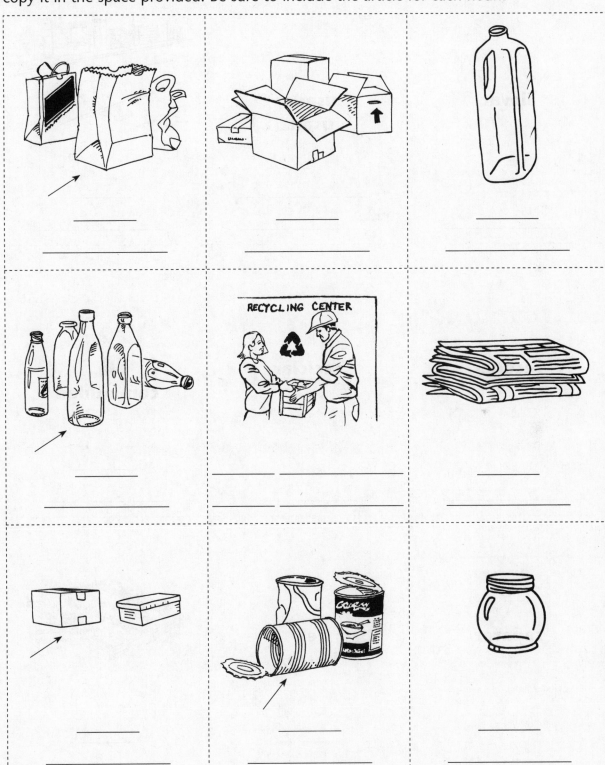

Realidades **B**

Capítulo 8B

Nombre _____

Hora _____

Fecha _____

Vocabulary Flash Cards, Sheet 2

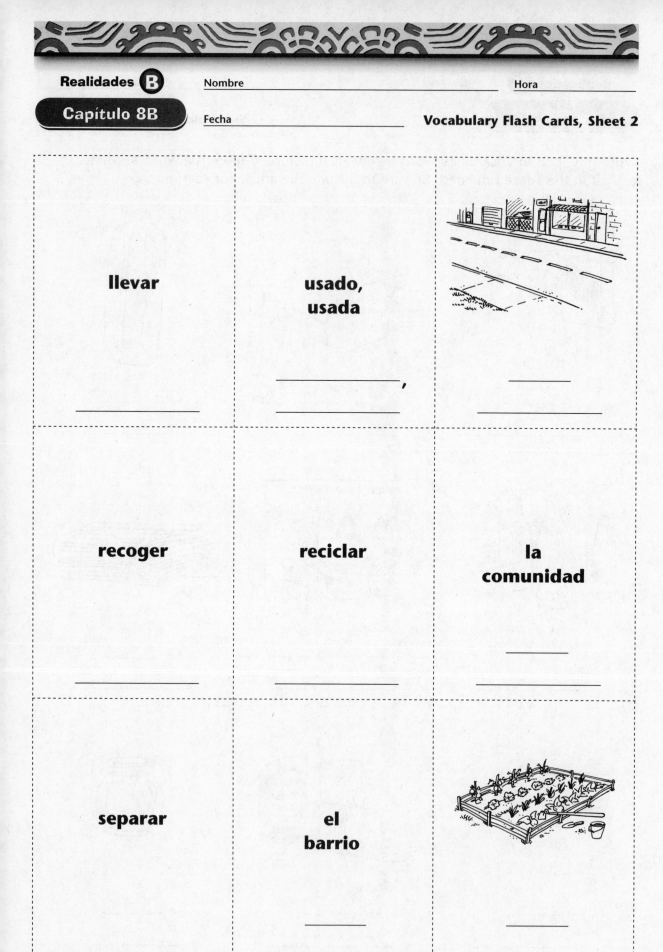

llevar

_____

usado,
usada

_____ ,

_____

recoger

_____

reciclar

_____

la
comunidad

_____

separar

_____

el
barrio

_____

_____

Realidades B

Capítulo 8B

Nombre _____

Hora _____

Fecha _____

Vocabulary Flash Cards, Sheet 3

_____

_____

la anciana

_____

_____

_____

_____

_____

_____

_____

la gente

_____

el anciano

_____

los demás

_____

_____

la
niña

los
niños

pobre

el
trabajo
voluntario

el
niño

el
problema

el voluntario,
la voluntaria

a menudo ___ _____	**la experiencia** ___ _____	**inolvidable** ___ _____
decidir ___ _____	**Hay que...** ___ _____	**¿Qué más?** ___ _____
Es necesario. ___ _____	**increíble** ___ _____	**la vez** ___ _____

Realidades **B**

Capítulo 8B

Nombre _____

Fecha _____

Hora _____

Vocabulary Flash Cards, Sheet 6

otra vez

_____

_____

_____

_____

decir

_____

_____

_____

_____

_____

_____

_____

_____

_____

_____

Realidades **B**

Nombre

Hora

Capítulo 8B

Fecha

Vocabulary Check, Sheet 1

Tear out this page. Write the English words on the lines. Fold the paper along the dotted line to see the correct answers so you can check your work.

la bolsa _____

la botella _____

la caja _____

el cartón _____

el centro de
reciclaje _____

la lata _____

llevar _____

_____

el periódico _____

el plástico _____

reciclar _____

recoger _____

_____

separar _____

usado, usada _____

el vidrio _____

el barrio _____

la calle _____

la comunidad _____

Fold In

Realidades Ⓑ

Capítulo 8B

Nombre _____

Hora _____

Fecha _____

Vocabulary Check, Sheet 2

Tear out this page. Write the Spanish words on the lines. Fold the paper along the dotted line to see the correct answers so you can check your work.

bag, sack _____

bottle _____

box _____

cardboard _____

recycling
center _____

can _____

to take;
to carry _____

newspaper _____

plastic _____

to recycle _____

to collect;
to gather _____

to separate _____

used _____

glass _____

neighborhood _____

street, road _____

community _____

Fold In ←

Tear out this page. Write the English words on the lines. Fold the paper along the dotted line to see the correct answers so you can check your work.

el jardín _____

el río _____

los ancianos _____

el campamento _____

los demás _____

la escuela primaria _____

la gente _____

el juguete _____

los niños _____

pobre _____

el proyecto de
construcción _____

el trabajo
voluntario _____

Fold In

Tear out this page. Write the Spanish words on the lines. Fold the paper along the dotted line to see the correct answers so you can check your work.

garden, yard   _____

river   _____

older people   _____

camp   _____

others   _____

primary school   _____

people   _____

toy   _____

children   _____

poor   _____

construction
project   _____

volunteer work   _____

_____

To hear a complete list of the vocabulary for this chapter, go to www.realidades.com and type in the Web Code jcd-0899. Then click on **Repaso del capítulo.**

Fold In

The present tense of *decir* (p. 262)

- **Decir** (*to say, to tell*) is irregular in the present tense. Here are its forms:

yo	**digo**	nosotros/nosotras	**decimos**
tú	**dices**	vosotros/vosotras	**decís**
usted/él/ella	**dice**	ustedes/ellos/ellas	**dicen**

- Notice that all the forms have an **i** in the stem except for the **nosotros/nosotras** and **vosotros/vosotras** forms (**decimos, decís**).

A. Write the correct forms of **decir** in the chart.

yo	nosotros/nosotras
tú	vosotros/vosotras decís
Ud./él/ella	Uds./ellos/ellas

B. Circle the correct forms of **decir** to complete each sentence.

1. Mis abuelos (**dicen** / **dice**) que el parque es bonito.

2. Yo (**dices** / **digo**) que es un video interesante.

3. Tú (**dices** / **dicen**) que el restaurante es bueno.

4. Ellos (**dice** / **dicen**) que la profesora es inteligente.

5. Nosotros (**dicen** / **decimos**) que el parque de diversiones es fantástico.

6. Ustedes (**digo** / **dicen**) que es divertido bucear.

7. Tú y yo (**dices** / **decimos**) que nos gusta pasear en bote.

C. Write complete sentences to find out what the people indicated say about a museum. Follow the model.

Modelo   Inés / decir que es fantástico

   Inés dice que es fantástico.

1. tú / decir que es aburrido _____

2. yo / decir que es interesante _____

3. ellos / decir que es divertido _____

4. nosotros / decir que es grande _____

5. Ud. / decir que es impresionante _____

realidades.com
- Web Code: jcd-0813

Realidades B

Capítulo 8B

Nombre _____

Hora _____

Fecha _____

Guided Practice Activities 8B-2

Indirect object pronouns (p. 264)

- An indirect object tells to whom or for whom an action is performed. In order to identify an indirect object, take the verb in the sentence and ask "For whom?" or "To whom?"

  Te traigo un recuerdo.   *I bring **you** a souvenir.*

  "To whom do I bring a souvenir?"   *"To **you**."*

- Indirect object pronouns must agree with the person they refer to.

	Singular		Plural
(yo)	**me** (to/for) me	**(nosotros)**	**nos** (to/for) us
(tú)	**te** (to/for) you (familiar)	**(vosotros)**	**os** (to/for) you
(Ud./él/ella)	**le** (to/for) you (formal), him, her	**(Uds./ellos/ellas)**	**les** (to/for) you (formal), them

- Like direct object pronouns, indirect object pronouns go before a conjugated verb.

  Te compré una tarjeta.   *I bought **you** a card.*

- When there is an infinitive with a conjugated verb, the indirect object pronoun can attach to the end of the infinitive or go before the conjugated verb.

  Me van a comprar una camiseta.   *They are going to buy **me** a T-shirt.*

  Van a comprar**me** una camiseta.   *They are going to buy **me** a T-shirt.*

A. Underline the indirect object pronoun in each sentence.

1. Te escribí una tarjeta.   4. Nos dan regalos.

2. Me trae un vaso de agua.   5. Les compramos una camiseta.

3. Le ayudo con la tarea.   6. Le llevamos unos libros.

B. Circle the correct indirect object pronoun. Follow the model.

Modelo   tú: ((Te) / Le) damos un boleto de avión.

1. yo: (Me / Nos) ayudan con la tarea.

2. tú: (Te / Les) llevo un regalo.

3. ella: (Le / Les) escribo una tarjeta.

4. nosotros: (Nos / Les) compraron unos zapatos.

5. ellos: (Le / Les) trae un vaso de agua.

6. él: (Le / Me) lavo el coche.

7. tú: (Me / Te) damos unas flores.

8. tú y yo: (Me / Nos) traen un recuerdo de las vacaciones.

realidades.com
- Web Code: jcd-0815

Indirect object pronouns (continued)

C. Write the correct indirect object pronoun in each sentence. Follow the model.

Modelo yo: _____Me_____ traen el periódico.

1. yo: _____ ayudan a limpiar el baño.

2. tú: _____ compran una sudadera.

3. él: _____ dan una bicicleta nueva.

4. nosotros: _____ traen unas cajas de cartón.

5. Ud.: _____ escriben una tarjeta.

6. ellos: _____ compro unos platos.

7. tú y yo: _____ traen una pizza grande.

8. Uds.: _____ compro un boleto de avión.

9. yo: _____ traen un vaso de jugo.

10. tú: _____ dan unos juguetes.

D. Write sentences to say to whom Susana is telling the truth. Follow the model.

Modelo yo _Susana me dice la verdad._

1. tú _____

2. él _____

3. nosotros _____

4. ellos _____

5. ella _____

6. tú y yo _____

7. ustedes _____

The preterite of *hacer* and *dar* (p. 266)

- The verbs **hacer** (*to make, to do*) and **dar** (*to give*) are irregular in the preterite.

hacer

yo	hice	nosotros/nosotras	hicimos
tú	hiciste	vosotros/vosotras	hicisteis
usted/él/ella	hizo	ustedes/ellos/ellas	hicieron

dar

yo	di	nosotros/nosotras	dimos
tú	diste	vosotros/vosotras	disteis
usted/él/ella	dio	ustedes/ellos/ellas	dieron

- These verbs have no accent marks in the preterite forms.
- Notice the change from **c** to **z** in the **usted/él/ella** form of **hacer: hizo.**

A. Write the missing forms of **hacer** and **dar** in the chart.

	hacer	dar
yo	hice	
tú		diste
Ud./él/ella		dio
nosotros/nosotras	hicimos	
Uds./ellos/ellas		dieron

B. Circle the correct forms of **hacer** and **dar** for each subject pronoun.

1. tú (**diste / dio**), (**hizo / hiciste**)

2. yo (**dio / di**), (**hice / hicimos**)

3. tú y yo (**dimos / diste**), (**hizo / hicimos**)

4. ellas (**di / dieron**), (**hice / hicieron**)

5. él (**diste / dio**), (**hizo / hice**)

6. Ud. (**di / dio**), (**hizo / hiciste**)

C. Complete each sentence with the correct form of the verb indicated. Follow the model. The boldfaced word is the subject of the sentence.

Modelo   **Ella** me (dar) _____*dio*_____ un libro.

1. **Tú** me (dar) _____ un regalo bonito.

2. **Ellos** me (hacer) _____ un suéter fantástico.

3. **Nosotros** te (dar) _____ unos discos compactos.

4. **Ud.** me (hacer) _____ un pastel sabroso.

realidades.com ✓
- Web Code: jcd-0814

Realidades B

Nombre _____

Hora _____

Capítulo 8B

Fecha _____

Guided Practice Activities 8B-5

Lectura: Hábitat para la Humanidad Internacional (pp. 272–273)

A. Recognizing cognates has helped you understand many of the readings in your textbook. The reading on Habitat for Humanity is no exception. Look at the words below and write their English equivalents in the spaces provided.

1. organización _____

2. internacional _____

3. comunidades _____

4. donaciones _____

5. privadas _____

6. miembros _____

B. Answer the following questions in Spanish in order to understand the main idea of the reading in your textbook.

1. ¿Qué es Hábitat y qué hace? Hábitat es una _____

_____ .

2. ¿Cuál es el objetivo de Hábitat? Su objetivo es _____

_____ .

3. ¿Cuántos proyectos en total tiene Hábitat en el mundo? Hábitat tiene _____

_____ .

C. Now, read the following passage to get more specific information about a typical Habitat project. Answer the questions that follow.

> *Según Hábitat, las personas pobres tienen que ayudar a construir sus casas. Es una manera positiva de ayudar a los demás. Hábitat les da los materiales de construcción y los trabajadores voluntarios.*

1. According to Habitat, who has to help build the houses? _____

_____

2. Who gives these people materials? _____

_____

3. Who else helps build the houses? _____

_____

4. Why do you think Habitat has such success? _____

_____

_____

Presentación escrita (p. 275)

Task: Imagine that you have to organize a clean-up campaign for a park, recreation center, school playground, or other place in your community. Make a poster announcing the project and inviting students to participate.

❶ **Prewrite.** Answer the following questions about your project:

a) ¿Qué van a limpiar ustedes?

_____

b) ¿Dónde está el lugar?

_____

c) ¿Qué tienen que hacer para preparar a limpiar?

_____

d) ¿Qué día van a trabajar?

_____

e) ¿Cuántas horas van a trabajar?

_____

f) ¿Quién(es) puede(n) participar?

_____

❷ **Draft.** Your answers to the questions above will determine what you say in your rough draft. Write your answers on a separate sheet of paper and organize them so that they will be easy to read and understand. You should also include any drawings, photos, or useful magazine cutouts you can find as part of your poster.

❸ **Revise.** Check your rough draft to make sure it is what you want. Your partner will check your work. Look on page 419 of your textbook to see what he or she will check.

❹ **Publish.** Take your partner's suggestions and do the changes necessary to make your poster as complete and effective as you can. Since you are now working on your final draft, your writing should be neat and your presentation should be on a clean poster. Your work may be presented in the classroom or even on the walls elsewhere in school, so make it look attractive!

Write the Spanish vocabulary word below each picture. If there is a word or phrase, copy it in the space provided. Be sure to include the article for each noun.

el canal

Realidades B

Capítulo 9A

Nombre _____

Hora _____

Fecha _____

Vocabulary Flash Cards, Sheet 2

_____

_____

_____

_____

_____

_____

_____

_____

_____

_____

_____

_____

_____

_____

la actriz

_____

_____

Realidades **B**

Nombre _____

Hora _____

Capítulo 9A

Fecha _____

Vocabulary Flash Cards, Sheet 3

**cómico,
cómica**

_____,

_____

infantil

_____

**violento,
violenta**

_____,

_____

emocionante

_____

realista

_____

me aburre(n)

_____

_____

fascinante

_____

**tonto,
tonta**

_____,

_____

**me
interesa(n)**

_____

Realidades B

Capítulo 9A

Nombre _____

Hora _____

Fecha _____

Vocabulary Flash Cards, Sheet 4

dar

_____

terminar

_____

medio,
media

_____,

_____

durar

_____

más de

_____

¿Qué clase
de...?

_____ _____

empezar

_____

menos de

_____

acabar de

_____

aburrir _____	**faltar** _____	**antes de** _____ _____
doler _____	**interesar** _____	**casi** _____
encantar _____	**quedar** _____	**¿De veras?** _____

Realidades **B**

Capítulo 9A

Nombre

Hora

Fecha

Vocabulary Flash Cards, Sheet 6

especialmente

_____

ya

_____

_____

por eso

_____

_____

_____

sobre

_____

_____

_____

Tear out this page. Write the English words on the lines. Fold the paper along the dotted line to see the correct answers so you can check your work.

el canal   _____

el programa
de concursos   _____

el programa de
dibujos animados   _____

el programa
deportivo   _____

el programa de
entrevistas   _____

el programa de
la vida real   _____

el programa de
noticias   _____

el programa
educativo   _____

el programa
musical   _____

la telenovela   _____

la comedia   _____

el drama   _____

la película de
ciencia ficción   _____

Fold In

Realidades **B**

Capítulo 9A

Nombre _____

Hora _____

Fecha _____

Vocabulary Check, Sheet 2

Tear out this page. Write the English words on the lines. Fold the paper along the dotted line to see the correct answers so you can check your work.

channel   _____

game show   _____

                                 _____

cartoon show   _____

                                 _____

sports show   _____

                                 _____

interview show   _____

                                 _____

reality program   _____

                                 _____

news program   _____

                                 _____

educational
program   _____

musical
program   _____

                                 _____

soap opera   _____

comedy   _____

drama   _____

science fiction
movie   _____

                                 _____

Fold In →

Tear out this page. Write the English words on the lines. Fold the paper along the dotted line to see the correct answers so you can check your work.

la película de
horror   _____

la película
policíaca   _____
                          _____

la película
romántica   _____
                          _____

emocionante   _____

fascinante   _____

infantil   _____
                          _____

tonto, tonta   _____

violento, violenta   _____

el actor   _____

la actriz   _____

dar   _____

durar   _____

empezar   _____

terminar   _____

Fold In

Realidades B

Capítulo 9A

Nombre _____

Fecha _____

Hora _____

Vocabulary Check, Sheet 4

Tear out this page. Write the English words on the lines. Fold the paper along the dotted line to see the correct answers so you can check your work.

horror movie _____

_____

crime movie, mystery _____

_____

romantic movie _____

_____

touching _____

fascinating _____

for children; childish _____

silly, stupid _____

violent _____

actor _____

actress _____

to show _____

to last _____

to begin _____

to end _____

To hear a complete list of the vocabulary for this chapter, go to www.realidades.com and type in the Web Code jcd-0989. Then click on **Repaso del capítulo.**

Fold In

Acabar de + infinitive (p. 294)

- Use present-tense forms of **acabar** with an infinitive to say that you and others have just finished doing something.

  Acabo de tomar una siesta.   *I just took a nap.*

  Acabamos de patinar.   *We just went skating.*

- Here are the present-tense forms of **acabar**, which is a regular **-ar** verb.

yo	**acabo**	nosotros/nosotras	**acabamos**
tú	**acabas**	vosotros/vosotras	**acabáis**
usted/él/ella	**acaba**	ustedes/ellos/ellas	**acaban**

A. Write the correct forms of **acabar** in the chart.

yo	nosotros/nosotras	
tú	vosotros/vosotras	acabáis
Ud./él/ella	Uds./ellos/ellas	

B. Circle the correct form of **acabar** to complete each sentence.

1. Yo (**acaba** / **acabo**) de ver un programa de la vida real.

2. Tú (**acabas** / **acabamos**) de ir al cine.

3. Ellos (**acaban** / **acaba**) de ver un video.

4. Tú y yo (**acabas** / **acabamos**) de cambiar el canal.

5. Usted (**acabo** / **acaba**) de ver una película policíaca.

6. Nosotros (**acabas** / **acabamos**) de hablar de las comedias.

7. Ustedes (**acabamos** / **acaban**) de comprar un lector DVD.

C. Complete each sentence with an activity you recently finished. Use the activities from **part B** above for ideas.

1. Yo acabo de _____.

2. Mis amigos y yo acabamos de _____.

3. Mi profesor (profesora) acaba de _____.

4. Los estudiantes de la escuela acaban de _____.

Realidades B

Capítulo 9A

Nombre _____

Hora _____

Fecha _____

Guided Practice Activities 9A-2

Acabar de + infinitive *(continued)*

D. Complete the following conversations with the correct forms of **acabar**.

ADELA: Mis amigos y yo _____ de ver una película de horror.

ANA: ¿Sí? ¡Qué casualidad! Yo también _____ de ver una película de horror.

LUIS: ¿Tú _____ de ver las noticias?

MARCOS: Sí. ¿Y ustedes?

LUIS: Nosotros _____ de ver un programa de concursos.

E. Create complete sentences. Follow the model.

Modelo   Alejandra / acabar de / sacar la basura

   Alejandra acaba de sacar la basura.

1. Natalia / acabar de / dar de comer al gato

_____

2. yo / acabar de / lavar los platos

_____

3. ellos / acabar de / quitar la mesa

_____

4. tú y yo / acabar de / cortar el césped

_____

5. tú / acabar de / limpiar el baño

_____

6. Ud. / acabar de / pasar la aspiradora

_____

F. Complete each sentence with forms of **acabar de** to say what you and other people you know recently did.

1. Yo _____.

2. Mi familia _____.

3. Mis amigos y yo _____.

4. Los estudiantes de la escuela _____.

realidades.com
• Web Code: jcd-0903

Gustar and similar verbs (p. 296)

- **Gustar** (*to please*) is different from other verbs you've learned. It is only used in its *third person forms*: **gusta** and **gustan**.
- **Gustar** is used with *indirect object pronouns* (**me, te, le, nos,** and **les**).
- **Gustar** agrees with the *subject* of the sentence, which is the object or objects that are pleasing to someone.

    indirect object pronoun + <u>**gusta**</u> + <u>singular</u> subject:

    Me **gusta** esa **comedia**. *I like that comedy. (That comedy pleases me.)*

    indirect object pronoun + <u>**gustan**</u> + <u>plural</u> subject:

    Nos **gusta<u>n</u>** los **drama<u>s</u>**. *We like dramas. (Dramas please us.)*

- Some other verbs are similar to **gustar**:

aburrir (aburre/aburren) *(to bore)*:	Me **aburre** ese **programa**.
	Me **aburren** las **telenovelas**.
doler (duele/duelen) *(to hurt)*:	Te **duele** la **mano**.
	Te **duelen** los **pies**.
encantar (encanta/encantan) *(to like a lot)*:	Nos **encanta** el **teatro**.
	Nos **encantan** los **museos**.
faltar (falta/faltan) *(to lack, to be missing)*:	Les **falta** un **vaso**.
	Les **faltan** los **anteojos**.
interesar (interesa/interesan) *(to interest)*:	Me **interesa** la **literatura**.
	Me **interesan** las **ciencias**.
quedar (queda/quedan) *(to fit)*:	Te **queda** bien el **vestido**.
	Te **quedan** bien los **zapatos**.

A. Look at each sentence. Circle the subject and underline the form of **gustar**. Follow the model.

Modelo Te <u>gustan</u> los (programas) de noticias. *P*

1. Me gustan los programas de entrevista. _____
2. Nos gusta la telenovela nueva. _____
3. ¿Te gusta el canal de deportes? _____
4. Les gustan los programas de dibujos animados. _____
5. Le gustan los programas de la vida real. _____
6. Nos gusta el programa musical en el canal 27. _____

B. Now, go back to the sentences in **part A** and write an **S** if they are singular (**gusta** + singular subject) or a **P** if they are plural (**gustan** + plural subject).

Gustar and similar verbs *(continued)*

C. Circle the correct form of **gustar** to complete each sentence.

1. Nos (**gusta** / **gustan**) las ciudades grandes.

2. Te (**gusta** / **gustan**) los parques nacionales.

3. Les (**gusta** / **gustan**) el teatro.

4. Me (**gusta** / **gustan**) el parque de diversiones.

5. Le (**gusta** / **gustan**) los animales.

D. Write the correct form of **gustar** to complete each sentence.

1. Nos _____ los jeans.   **4.** Me _____ el traje.

2. Les _____ los zapatos.   **5.** Te _____ las botas.

3. Le _____ la gorra.   **6.** Les _____ el suéter.

E. These sentences use verbs that are similar to **gustar**. Circle the correct form for each verb.

1. Nos (**encanta** / **encantan**) las tiendas de ropa.

2. Me (**aburre** / **aburren**) los programas de la vida real.

3. Te (**duele** / **duelen**) los pies.

4. Les (**interesa** / **interesan**) los programas de noticias.

5. Le (**falta** / **faltan**) un cuchillo.

6. Me (**queda** / **quedan**) bien la falda.

F. Now write **a** or **an** to complete each of the following verbs.

1. Me encant_____ los programas de concursos.

2. Te interes_____ la nueva telenovela.

3. Nos falt_____ un vaso.

4. Me qued_____ bien la sudadera.

G. Write **e** or **en** to complete each of the following verbs.

1. Le aburr_____ los programas educativos.

2. Me duel_____ la cabeza.

3. Nos aburr_____ ese libro.

4. Te duel_____ el estómago.

• Web Code: jcd-0904

Realidades **B**

Nombre _____

Hora _____

Capítulo 9A

Fecha _____

Guided Practice Activities 9A-5

Lectura: Una semana sin televisión (pp. 300–301)

A. Read through the reading in your textbook without stopping to look up words in a dictionary. On a separate sheet of paper, make a list of any words you don't know. Then, answer the following questions about the reading in Spanish. If you have trouble with any of the words, look them up while you answer the questions.

1. ¿Qué dos cosas hacen los niños estadounidenses más que cualquier otra cosa?

_____ y _____

2. Según los estudios, ¿cuáles son tres resultados malos del ver demasiado la televisión?

_____, _____ y

_____

3. ¿Qué hacen millones de personas durante el mes de abril?

_____ .

B. Read through the reading in your textbook once more. If there are words or phrases you still do not understand, look them up in a dictionary. Now, answer the questions below circling **C** for **cierto** (*true*) and **F** for **falso** (*false*).

1. **C F** Según la lectura, los niños comen más que cualquier otra cosa, a excepción de dormir.

2. **C F** Ver demasiado la televisión puede resultar en un exceso de peso.

3. **C F** En cuatro horas de dibujos animados el sábado por la mañana, los niños pueden ver más de 200 anuncios sobre los deportes.

4. **C F** Hay estudios que dicen que los niños que ven demasiado la tele pueden tener más probabilidad de ser violentos y agresivos de adultos.

5. **C F** Para muchas familias en varios países una semana sin televisión les da la oportunidad de hacer cosas interesantes en vez de ver la tele.

C. You may have a discussion about the benefits and drawbacks of watching TV. Think of which argument you want to support. Then write three reasons in Spanish for why you feel this way. You can use information from the reading in your textbook or from personal experience.

Razón 1: _____

Razón 2: _____

Razón 3: _____

Presentación oral (p. 303)

Task: You are going to write a review of a movie or television show that was on your school's closed-circuit TV system. Prepare a summary of the movie or show.

A. Choose a movie or show to talk about. Fill in the chart with the information about your show or movie.

Nombre	
Clase de película o programa	
Actor/Actores	
Actriz/Actrices	
Cómo es	
Cuánto tiempo dura	
Para quiénes es	

B. Collect visuals to go along with your presentation. They could be ads or photos from a newspaper or magazine, such as a TV guide, or you could download pictures from the Internet. Make a poster with all of the items you collect.

C. Use the notes you took in **part A** to prepare your presentation. Write out complete sentences for each topic in the spaces below.

1. _____.
2. _____.
3. _____.
4. _____.
5. _____.
6. _____.
7. _____.

D. Now, put together your finished poster and your sentences and practice your presentation. Remember to:

_____ speak clearly

_____ use complete sentences

_____ provide all key information about the movie or show

Write the Spanish vocabulary word below each picture. If there is a word or phrase, copy it in the space provided. Be sure to include the article for each noun.

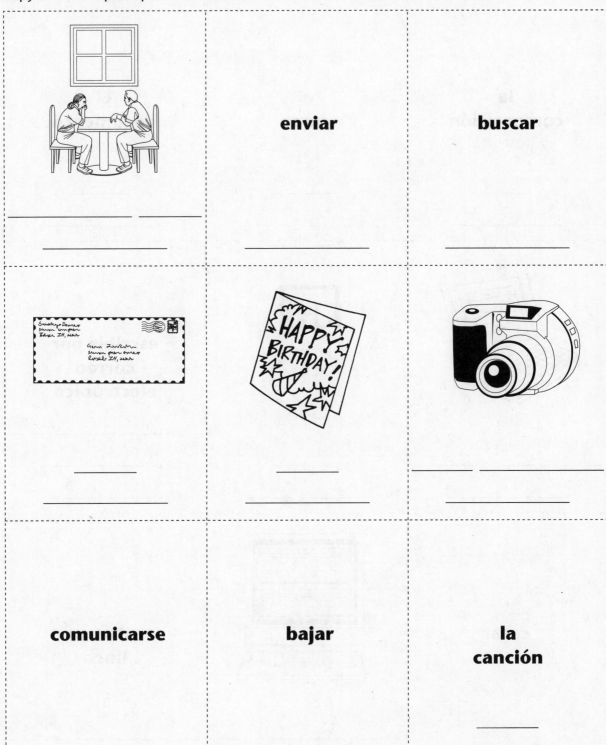

	enviar	buscar
comunicarse	bajar	la canción

Realidades **B**

Nombre _____

Hora _____

Capítulo 9B

Fecha _____

Vocabulary Flash Cards, Sheet 2

la
composición

_____

_____

el
curso

_____

_____

el
documento

_____

_____

_____

_____

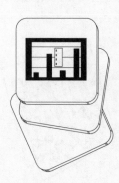

_____

_____

escribir por
correo
electrónico

_____

_____

crear

_____

_____

_____

_____

estar en
línea

_____

_____

Realidades **B**

Nombre _____

Hora _____

Capítulo 9B

Fecha _____

Vocabulary Flash Cards, Sheet 3

_____

_____ _____

**el
informe**

_____

_____

_____

_____

**los
gráficos**

_____

_____

**el
laboratorio**

_____

_____

**la
presentación**

_____

_____

**la
información**

_____

_____

_____

_____ _____

_____

_____

Realidades Ⓑ

Capítulo 9B

Nombre _____

Hora _____

Fecha _____

Vocabulary Flash Cards, Sheet 4

visitar salones de chat

_____

_____

¿Qué te parece?

_____

_____

tener miedo (de)

_____

_____

complicado, complicada

_____,

_____

rápidamente

_____

_____

conocer

_____

_____

¿Para qué sirve?

_____

_____

Sirve para...

_____

_____

saber

_____

_____

Tear out this page. Write the English words on the lines. Fold the paper along the dotted line to see the correct answers so you can check your work.

cara a cara _____

la carta _____

comunicarse _____

_____

enviar _____

la tarjeta _____

bajar _____

buscar _____

la cámara
digital _____

_____

la canción _____

la composición _____

la computadora
portátil _____

_____

crear _____

el curso _____

la diapositiva _____

la dirección
electrónica _____

el documento _____

Fold In →

Realidades B

Capítulo 9B

Nombre

Fecha

Hora

Vocabulary Check, Sheet 2

Tear out this page. Write the Spanish words on the lines. Fold the paper along the dotted line to see the correct answers so you can check your work.

face-to-face _____

letter _____

to communicate (with) _____

to send _____

card _____

to download _____

to search (for) _____

digital camera _____

_____

song _____

composition _____

laptop computer _____

_____

to create _____

course _____

slide _____

e-mail address _____

_____

document _____

Fold In

Tear out this page. Write the English words on the lines. Fold the paper along the dotted line to see the correct answers so you can check your work.

escribir por
correo electrónico   _____
    _____

estar en línea   _____

grabar un disco
compacto   _____

los gráficos   _____

la información   _____

el informe   _____

el laboratorio   _____

navegar en la Red   _____

la presentación   _____

el sitio Web   _____

visitar salones
de chat   _____
    _____

Fold In

Tear out this page. Write the Spanish words on the lines. Fold the paper along the dotted line to see the correct answers so you can check your work.

to send an
e-mail message
_____
_____

to be online
_____

to burn a CD
_____
_____

graphics
_____

information
_____

report
_____

laboratory
_____

to surf the Web
_____

presentation
_____

Web site
_____

to visit
chat rooms
_____
_____

To hear a complete list of the vocabulary for this chapter,
go to www.realidades.com and type in the Web Code jcd-0999.
Then click on **Repaso del capítulo.**

Fold In

Realidades **B**

Nombre _____

Hora _____

Capítulo 9B

Fecha _____

Guided Practice Activities 9B-1

The present tense of *pedir* and *servir* (p. 320)

- You have learned other verbs with stem changes in the present tense (**pensar, querer, preferir**), where the stem changes from **e** to **ie**.

- **Pedir** (t*o ask for*) and **servir** (*to serve, or to be useful for*) are also stem-changing verbs in the present tense, but their stem changes from **e** to **i**.

- Here are the present tense forms of **pedir** and **servir**. Notice that the **nosotros/ nosotras** and **vosotros/vosotras** forms do not change their stem.

yo	<u>pi</u>do	nosotros/nosotras	pedimos
tú	<u>pi</u>des	vosotros/vosotras	pedís
usted/él/ella	<u>pi</u>de	ustedes/ellos/ellas	<u>pi</u>den

yo	<u>sir</u>vo	nosotros/nosotras	servimos
tú	<u>sir</u>ves	vosotros/vosotras	servís
usted/él/ella	<u>sir</u>ve	ustedes/ellos/ellas	<u>sir</u>ven

A. Complete the chart with the correct forms of **pedir** and **servir**.

	pedir	servir
yo	pido	
tú		sirves
Ud./él/ella		
nosotros/nosotras		
Uds./ellos/ellas		

B. Write **e** or **i** in the blank to complete each verb form.

1. yo p_____do

2. tú s_____rves

3. nosotros s_____rvimos

4. ellos p_____den

5. Ud. s_____rve

6. ellos s_____rven

7. nosotros p_____dimos

8. ella s_____rve

9. yo s_____rvo

10. tú p_____des

Realidades B

Capítulo 9B

Nombre _____

Hora _____

Fecha _____

Guided Practice Activities 9B-2

The present tense of *pedir* and *servir (continued)*

C. Circle the correct form of **pedir** or **servir** to complete each sentence.

1. Tú (**sirve** / **sirves**) café con leche y unas galletas.

2. Yo (**pido** / **pedimos**) una hamburguesa con papas fritas para el almuerzo.

3. Nosotros (**pido** / **pedimos**) un jugo de naranja.

4. Este libro (**sirves** / **sirve**) para aprender química.

5. Ellos (**pedimos** / **piden**) un tenedor limpio.

6. Todos los domingos mi madre (**sirve** / **sirven**) pescado para la cena.

7. Tú y yo (**pido** / **pedimos**) ayuda con la computadora.

8. Las computadoras (**sirven** / **servimos**) para conectar los sitios Web.

D. Write the correct form of the verb in the blank. Follow the model.

Modelo Yo siempre (**pedir**)_____*pido*_____ yogur para el desayuno.

1. Mis amigos (**servir**) _____ café con el postre.

2. Nosotros siempre (**pedir**) _____ café con leche.

3. Las computadoras (**servir**) _____ para navegar la Red.

4. Tú y yo (**servir**) _____ jugo de naranja con una ensalada de frutas.

5. Tú siempre (**pedir**) _____ pizza para la cena.

6. Mis hermanos siempre (**pedir**) _____ huevos para el desayuno.

E. Complete the following sentences in a logical manner. Follow the models for ideas.

Modelos Los bolígrafos (**servir**)_____*sirven para escribir*_____.

En el restaurante mexicano, yo siempre (**pedir**)_____*pido enchiladas*_____.

1. Mi computadora (**servir**) _____

_____.

2. Para el desayuno, yo siempre (**pedir**) _____

_____.

3. Para el almuerzo, la cafetería siempre (**servir**) _____

_____.

4. Cuando vamos a un restaurante, mis amigos y yo (**pedir**) _____

_____.

Saber and conocer (p. 324)

- Both these verbs are irregular in the **yo** form only. Here are their present-tense forms.

yo	**sé**	nosotros/nosotras	**sabemos**
tú	**sabes**	vosotros/vosotras	**sabéis**
usted/él/ella	**sabe**	ustedes/ellos/ellas	**saben**

yo	**conozco**	nosotros/nosotras	**conocemos**
tú	**conoces**	vosotros/vosotras	**conocéis**
usted/él/ella	**conoce**	ustedes/ellos/ellas	**conocen**

A. Write the missing forms of **saber** and **conocer** in the chart.

	saber	conocer
yo	sé	
tú		
Ud./él/ella		
nosotros/nosotras		conocemos
Uds./ellos/ellas		

- Both **saber** and **conocer** mean *to know*.
- **Saber** means *to know how to do something* or *to know a fact*:
    Ella **sabe patinar**.   *She **knows how to skate**.*
    Él **sabe la respuesta**.   *He **knows the answer**.*
- **Conocer** means *to know a person* or *to be familiar with a place or thing*. Remember to use the personal **a** with **conocer** when it is used with a person.
    Ella **conoce Madrid**.   *She **knows (is familiar with)** Madrid.*
    Él **conoce a Miguel**.   *He **knows Miguel**.*

B. Look at each person, place, or thing. Write **S** if you would use **saber** or **C** if you would use **conocer**. Follow the model.

Modelo ___S___ las matemáticas

1. _____ la profesora de español
2. _____ nadar
3. _____ tocar la guitarra

4. _____ Tokyo
5. _____ Britney Spears
6. _____ la respuesta correcta

Realidades B

Capítulo 9B

Nombre _____

Hora _____

Fecha _____

Guided Practice Activities 9B-4

Saber and *conocer* (continued)

C. Circle the correct verb form of **conocer** in each sentence.

1. Yo (**conoce** / **conozco**) una tienda muy buena para comprar ropa.

2. Ellos (**conoces** / **conocen**) muy bien la ciudad de Nueva York.

3. Ella (**conoce** / **conozco**) a todos los estudiantes de la clase.

4. Tú y yo (**conocemos** / **conozco**) la música de Carlos Santana.

D. Circle the correct form of **saber** in each sentence.

1. Nosotros (**saben** / **sabemos**) hablar español.

2. Yo (**sabe** / **sé**) la respuesta correcta.

3. Tú (**sabes** / **sabe**) dónde está la clase de matemáticas.

4. Ud. (**sabes** / **sabe**) esquiar y nadar.

E. Complete each sentence with a form of **saber** or **conocer**. Circle the correct verb form according to the context.

1. Tú y yo (**sabemos** / **conocemos**) tocar el piano.

2. Ellas (**saben** / **conocen**) dónde están las llaves.

3. Yo (**sé** / **conozco**) al presidente de los Estados Unidos.

4. Tú (**sabes** / **conoces**) bien la ciudad de Chicago.

5. Ud. (**sabe** / **conoce**) usar la computadora nueva.

6. Nosotros (**sabemos** / **conocemos**) el nombre de una canción en español.

7. Tú (**sabes** / **conoces**) a todos los estudiantes de la clase.

8. Uds. (**saben** / **conocen**) a la estudiante nueva.

F. Complete the following sentences. Use ideas from the activities above or other words you know. Follow the model.

Modelo Yo (saber) _____*sé montar en bicicleta*_____ .

1. Yo (saber) _____ .

2. Yo no (saber) _____ .

3. Yo (conocer) _____ .

4. Yo no (conocer) _____ .

realidades.com
• Web Code: jcd-0914

Realidades B

Nombre _____

Hora _____

Capítulo 9B

Fecha _____

Guided Practice Activities 9B-5

Lectura: La invasión del ciberspanglish (pp. 328–329)

A. The article in your textbook talks about the influence of computers on language. What computer terms can you think of in English? Write ten words or phrases that are commonly used when talking about the computer or the Internet. The first two have been done for you.

1. _surf the Web_
2. _to download_
3. _____
4. _____
5. _____

6. _____
7. _____
8. _____
9. _____
10. _____

B. Did you find words in the reading similar to those on your list? You may have found the *ciberspanglish* words as well as the more correct Spanish terms for each word. Look on the chart in your reading and find the *ciberspanglish* and Spanish words for each.

	Ciberspanglish	**Español**
1. to chat	_____	_____
2. to reboot	_____	_____
3. to program	_____	_____
4. clip art	_____	_____
5. to print	_____	_____

C. Which list has the longer words in **part B**? Read the excerpts from the reading in your textbook. Then, write in English why some people want to use *ciberspanglish* terms and why some people prefer to use Spanish terms for computer-related words.

> *A algunas personas no les gusta nada este nuevo "idioma". Piensan que el español es suficientemente rico para poder traducir los términos del inglés.*
>
> *Hay otros que dicen que no hay problemas con mezclar los idiomas para comunicarse mejor. Piensan que el "ciberspanglish" es más fácil y lógico porque los términos técnicos vienen del inglés y expresarlos en español es bastante complicado.*

1. It is better to use Spanish because _____

_____.

2. It is better to use *ciberspanglish* because _____

_____.

realidades.com

• Web Code: jcd-0915

Presentación escrita (p. 331)

Task: Pretend that your parents think you spend too much time at the computer. Write an e-mail to a friend in Mexico defending your computer use.

❶ Prewrite. Fill in the chart below. In the first column, write in Spanish three ways you use the computer. In the second column, write the benefit (**ventaja**) to you. Use the first example as a guide.

Cómo uso la computadora	La ventaja
Busco información para mis clases, en Internet.	*Aprendo mucho y es muy interesante.*

❷ Draft. Use the information from the chart to write your e-mail.

❸ Revise. Before you have a partner review your work, check for spelling, accent marks, correct vocabulary use, and verb forms. Your partner will review the following:

_____ Is the paragraph easy to read and understand?

_____ Does the paragraph provide good reasons and support your position?

_____ Is there anything that you could add to give more information?

_____ Is there anything that you could change to make it clearer?

_____ Are there any errors that you missed?

❹ Publish. Rewrite the e-mail making any change suggested by your partner or by changing anything you didn't like.

❺ Evaluation. Your teacher will grade you on the following:

- the amount of information provided
- how well you presented each reason and its benefit
- your use of vocabulary and accuracy of spelling and grammar

Fecha _____

Vocabulary Flash Cards

Fecha _____ **Vocabulary Flash Cards**

Fecha _____   **Vocabulary Flash Cards**

Prentice Hall Realidades B

Leveled Vocabulary and Grammar Workbook
Core Practice

PEARSON

Boston, Massachusetts   Chandler, Arizona   Glenview, Illinois   Upper Saddle River, New Jersey

ISBN-13: 978-0-13-369267-9

ISBN-10: 0-13-369267-1

15 16

PEARSON

Table of Contents

Realidades **B**

Capítulo 5A

Nombre _____

Fecha _____

Hora _____

Core Practice **5A–1**

La familia

A. Patricia is telling you about her family. Label each person in her family tree with a word that describes his or her relationship to Patricia. You may use some words more than once.

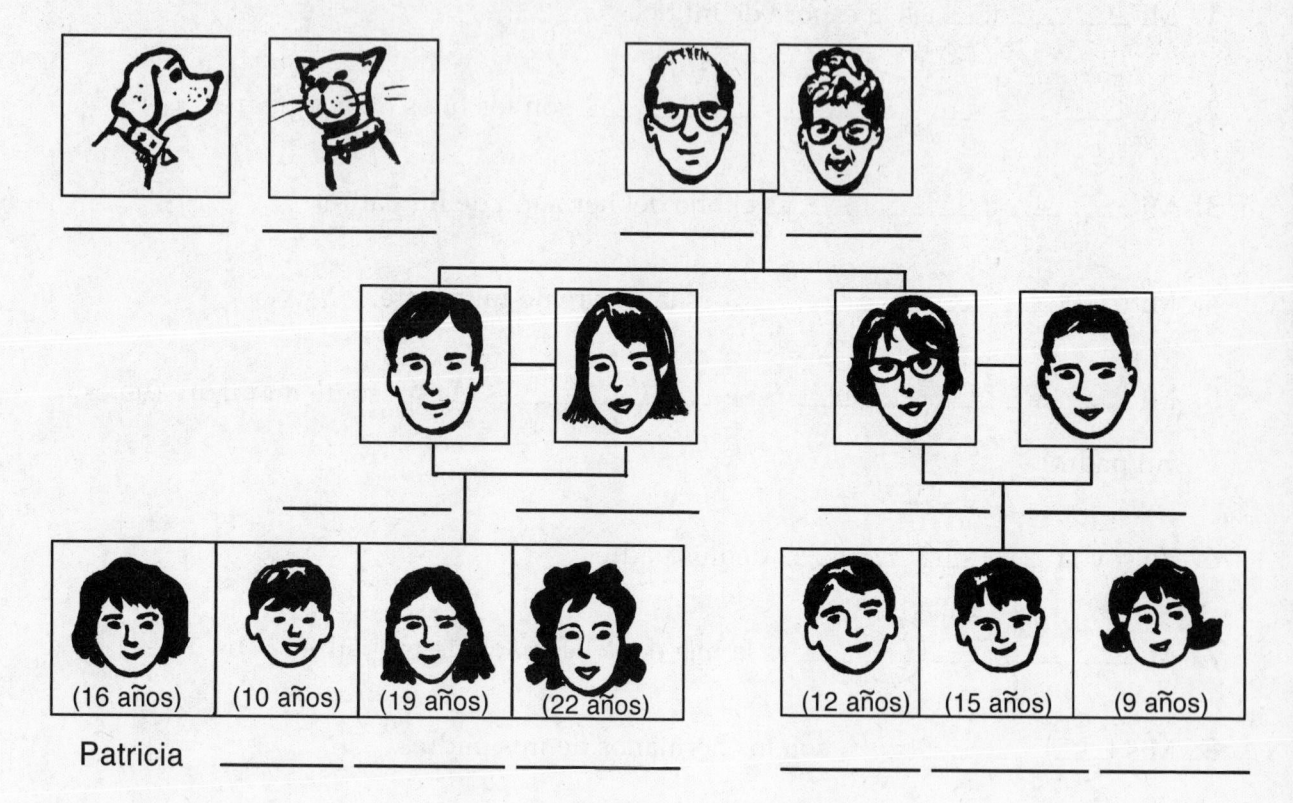

(16 años) (10 años) (19 años) (22 años)   (12 años) (15 años) (9 años)

Patricia _____ _____ _____   _____ _____ _____

B. Now, answer the following questions by circling **sí** or **no**.

1. ¿Patricia tiene hermanastros?   Sí   No

2. ¿Patricia tiene hermanas mayores?   Sí   No

3. ¿Patricia tiene dieciséis años?   Sí   No

4. ¿Patricia tiene tres primos menores?   Sí   No

5. ¿Patricia tiene dos abuelas?   Sí   No

Realidades B

Capítulo 5A

Nombre _____

Fecha _____

Hora _____

Core Practice **5A–2**

¿Quién es?

A. Complete the sentences below with the correct family relationships.

1. Mi ___ ___ (⎯) es la esposa de mi tío.

2. Mis ___ ___ ___ (⎯) ___ ___ ___ ___ son los hijos de mis padres.

3. Mi ___ ___ (⎯) ___ ___ es el hijo del hermano de mi padre.

4. Mi (⎯) ___ ___ ___ ___ ___ ___ es la madre de mi madre.

5. Mi ___ ___ ___ ___ ___ ___ ___ (⎯) ___ es el esposo de mi madre (no es mi padre).

6. Yo soy la ___ ___ ___ (⎯) de mis padres.

7. Mi ___ ___ ___ (⎯) ___ es la hija de la hermana de mi padre.

8. Mis (⎯) ___ ___ ___ son los hermanos de mis padres.

9. Mamá y papá son mis ___ ___ (⎯) ___ ___ ___ .

10. Mis ___ ___ (⎯) ___ ___ ___ ___ (⎯) ___ ___ ___ son las hijas de la esposa de mi padre (no son mis hermanas).

B. Now, unscramble the circled letters to come up with another member of the family.

___ ___ ___ ___ ___ ___ ___ ___ ___ ___ ___ ___ ___

realidades.com ✔
• Web Code: jcd-0501

Realidades **B**

Capítulo 5A

Nombre _____

Hora _____

Fecha _____

Core Practice **5A–3**

¡Una fiesta inesperada (*a surprise party*)!

The Rodríguez family is giving their older son Tomás a surprise birthday party. Complete their conversation, using the most logical word from the word bank.

luces	la piñata	tiene	decoraciones
dulces	pastel	celebrar	sólo
globos	sacar fotos	regalos	

MAMÁ: Vamos a hacer el plan porque vamos a _____ el cumpleaños

de Tomás. Él _____ doce años.

TÍA LULÚ: Sí, ¡vamos a celebrar! Primero, necesitamos un _____ para

comer ¿no? ¡Qué sabroso!

MAMÁ: Sí. Y necesitamos unas _____ perfectas. Vamos a necesitar un

globo y una luz.

TÍA LULÚ: ¿_____ *un* globo y *una* luz? ¡No, necesitamos muchos

_____ y muchas _____! También

necesitamos papel picado.

PABLITO: Oye, ¡yo tengo una cámara fabulosa! Puedo _____ en la fiesta

cuando Tomás abre los _____.

MAMÁ: Sí, Pablito. ¡Muchas gracias! Y finalmente, pueden romper

_____. ¿Tenemos _____?

TÍA LULÚ: Sí, tenemos muchos dulces.

PABLITO: ¡Qué buena fiesta!

La celebración

Raúl is explaining how he and his family are preparing for his sister's birthday party. Read his description and answer the questions that follow in complete sentences.

> Hoy es el cumpleaños de mi hermana menor, Gabriela. Mis padres y yo preparamos la fiesta. Mi mamá decora con el papel picado y las luces. Mi papá tiene los regalos y los globos. Yo preparo la mesa con los globos y el pastel. También tengo la cámara porque voy a hacer un video de la fiesta.
>
> Sólo nuestra familia va a estar aquí, pero con todos mis primos, mis tíos y mis abuelos tenemos muchas personas. A las cinco mi hermana va a estar aquí y la fiesta va a empezar.

1. ¿Quién es Gabriela? _____

2. ¿Para quién es la fiesta? _____

3. ¿Qué clase de fiesta es? _____

4. ¿Con qué decora Raúl? _____

5. ¿Qué tiene el papá? _____

6. ¿Qué va a hacer Raúl? _____

7. ¿Quiénes van a estar en la fiesta? _____

_____

8. ¿A qué hora va a empezar la fiesta? _____

Realidades Ⓑ

Capítulo 5A

Nombre _____

Hora _____

Fecha _____

Core Practice **5A–5**

Conversaciones

You overhear a group of students talking. Fill in the blanks in their conversations with the correct forms of the verb **tener**.

1. FRANCO: Hola, Carmen. ¿Qué tienes en la mano?

CARMEN: (Yo) _____ un regalo para mi primo. Es su cumpleaños.

FRANCO: Ah, ¿sí? ¿Cuántos años _____?

CARMEN: _____ doce años.

FRANCO: Mis primos también _____ doce años.

2. ELENA: ¡Oye, Carlos! ¿Cuántos años _____?

CARLOS: ¿Yo? Yo _____ quince años. ¿Por qué?

ELENA: Porque mi hermano y yo _____ una prima de quince

años que _____ que ir a un baile el viernes. ¿(Tú)

_____ planes?

CARLOS: ¿El viernes? No, no _____ otros planes.

3. PABLO: Hola, José. Hola, Manolo. ¿(Uds.) _____ un dólar?

JOSÉ: Sí, yo _____ un dólar. ¿Por qué?

PABLO: Porque yo _____ hambre y quiero comprar un perrito

caliente.

MANOLO: ¿La cafetería _____ perritos calientes buenos?

PABLO: Sí. ¿Quieres uno?

JOSÉ: Sí, pero primero Manolo y yo _____ que ir a clase.

PABLO: También _____ que ir a clase.

Realidades B

Capítulo 5A

Nombre _____

Fecha _____

Hora _____

Core Practice **5A–6**

¿De quién es?

A. Fill in the following chart with the masculine and feminine, singular and plural forms of the possessive adjectives indicated.

hijo	tía	abuelos	hermanas
			mis hermanas
	tu tía		
su hijo			
		nuestros abuelos	
vuestro hijo	*vuestra tía*	*vuestros abuelos*	*vuestras hermanas*

B. Now, complete the following sentences by writing in the possessive adjective that corresponds with the English adjective in parentheses. Follow the model.

Modelo (*my*) _____Mi_____ abuela es vieja.

1. (*our*) _____ abuelos van a la casa para hablar con nosotros.

2. (*your*) Sara, gracias por _____ libro.

3. (*my*) _____ prima es de Tejas.

4. (*your*) ¿Tienen mucha tarea en _____ clase de matemáticas?

5. (*their*) _____ tíos están en la oficina ahora.

6. (*my*) El perro come _____ galletas.

7. (*our*) Nosotros vamos a la escuela en _____ bicicletas.

8. (*your*) Profesor, ¿dónde está _____ oficina?

9. (*their*) _____ hijo es muy trabajador.

10. (*his*) _____ hermana está enferma.

realidades.com

• Web Code: jcd-0505

Realidades B

Capítulo 5A

Nombre _____

Fecha _____

Hora _____

Core Practice **5A–7**

La fiesta perfecta

Using the subjects below and the activities suggested by the pictures, write complete sentences about what your friends and relatives have for the party. Make sure you use the correct possessive adjective. Follow the model.

Mi primo Juan

Modelo *Mi primo Juan tiene su cámara.*

Mis tíos

1. _____

Alicia

2. _____

Tú

3. _____

Nosotros

4. _____

Yo

5. _____

Ud.

6. _____

La profesora Méndez

7. _____

Nosotras

8. _____

Realidades B

Capítulo 5A

Nombre _____

Fecha _____

Hora _____

Core Practice **5A–8**

Repaso

Across

5. La madre de mi primo es mi _____.

7. El hermano de mi padre es mi _____.

9. *sister*

11.

13. mi papá; el _____

16. La mamá de mi padre es mi _____.

17. Mi hermano y yo somos los _____ de nuestros padres.

19.

20.

21. mi mamá; la _____

Down

1. El esposo de mi madre; no es mi papá, es mi _____.

2. *brother*

3.

4. el papel _____

6.

8. ¡Feliz _____! ¿Cuántos años tienes?

9. Quiero _____ un video.

10. la madre de mi hermanastro; mi _____

12. Los hijos _____ la piñata.

14. Es el hermano de mi prima; mi _____.

15. ¿Quién _____ las fotos de la fiesta?

18. *parents*

21. no menor

Realidades B

Capítulo 5A

Nombre _____

Fecha _____

Hora _____

Core Practice **5A–9**

Organizer

I. Vocabulary

To describe family relationships

_____

_____

_____

_____

_____

_____

_____

Activities at a party

_____

_____

_____

_____

Items at a party

_____

_____

_____

_____

_____

Words to express possession

_____

_____

_____

_____

_____

II. Grammar

1. The forms of **tener** are: _____ _____

   _____ _____

   _____ _____

2. Possessive adjectives in Spanish are written as follows:

	Singular/Plural			Singular/Plural	
my	_____ / _____		our	_____ / _____	
your (familiar)	_____ / _____		your (pl., familiar)	_____ / _____	
your (formal), his, hers	_____ / _____		your (pl., formal), their	_____ / _____	

Realidades **B**

Capítulo 5B

Nombre _____

Fecha _____

Hora _____

Core Practice **5B–1**

Restaurante elegante

Label the following items with the correct word. Don't forget to use the correct definite article (**el** or **la**).

1. _____   5. _____   9. _____

2. _____   6. _____   10. _____

3. _____   7. _____   11. _____

4. _____   8. _____

realidades.com
• Web Code: jcd-0511

Realidades B

Capítulo 5B

Nombre _____

Hora _____

Fecha _____

Core Practice **5B–2**

Las descripciones

You are telling your friends about some of your family members. Write descriptions of them in complete sentences. Follow the model.

6'5"

Paco

Modelo

Paco es alto y tiene el pelo corto y negro.

6'4"

El tío Roberto

1. _____
   _____
   _____

5'0"

Melinda, mi madrastra

2. _____
   _____
   _____

5'2"

El abuelito Jorge

3. _____
   _____
   _____

6'2"

Los primos Juan y Manuel

4. _____
   _____
   _____

5'10"

Esperanza

5. _____
   _____
   _____

Realidades **B**

Capítulo 5B

Nombre _____

Fecha _____

Hora _____

Core Practice **5B–3**

La palabra correcta

Complete the following mini-conversations with the most logical words or phrases from your vocabulary.

1. — ¿Necesita Ud. algo?

    — Sí, me _____ un tenedor.

2. — ¿Te gusta la comida del Sr. Vargas?

    — Sí, es deliciosa. ¡Qué _____!

3. — ¿Quieres otra _____ de café?

    — No, gracias.

4. — ¿Desea Ud. un té helado?

    — Sí, porque tengo _____.

5. — ¿Qué vas a _____ de postre?

    — Yo quiero el flan.

6. — ¿Necesitan _____ más?

    — Sí, la cuenta por favor.

7. — Muchas gracias.

    — De _____.

8. — ¿Qué quisiera Ud. de _____ _____?

    — Me gustaría el arroz con pollo.

9. — ¿Estás cansado?

    — Sí, tengo _____.

10. — ¿Bebes el café?

    — Sí, porque tengo _____.

realidades.com
• Web Code: jcd-0512

Realidades **B**

Capítulo 5B

Nombre _____

Hora _____

Fecha _____

Core Practice **5B-4**

Cita (*date*) en español

A. David and Rocío are on a date at a Spanish restaurant. Using the vocabulary you have learned in this chapter, write their possible responses to the waiter's questions. Use complete sentences.

CAMARERO: ¿Qué desean Uds. de plato principal?

DAVID: _____

ROCÍO: _____

CAMARERO: ¿Cómo está la comida?

DAVID: _____

ROCÍO: _____

CAMARERO: ¿Desean algo más?

DAVID: _____

ROCÍO: _____

B. Now, based on the waiter's responses, write what you think David or Rocío may have asked the waiter.

DAVID: ¿ _____ ?

CAMARERO: Sí, le traigo una servilleta.

ROCÍO: ¿ _____ ?

CAMARERO: Sí, ahora puede pedir algo de postre.

DAVID: ¿ _____ ?

CAMARERO: Un café, por supuesto. ¿Tiene sueño?

Realidades B

Capítulo 5B

Nombre _____

Fecha _____

Hora _____

Core Practice **5B-5**

¿Quién viene?

Your class has decided to put on a talent show, and you are in charge of scheduling what time everyone is coming to audition for different skits. Your friend Lola is anxious to know the schedule. Answer her questions using the picture below. Follow the model.

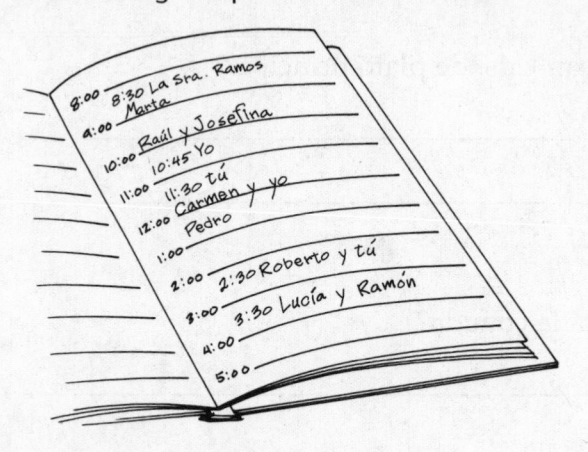

8:00   8:30 La Sra. Ramos
              Marta
9:00 Raúl y Josefina
10:00
        10:45 Yo
11:00
        11:30 tú
12:00 Carmen y yo
        Pedro
1:00
2:00   2:30 Roberto y tú
3:00   3:30 Lucía y Ramón
4:00
5:00

Modelo   ¿Quién viene a las ocho y media?
La Sra. Ramos viene a las ocho y media.

1. ¿Quién viene a las nueve?

   _____

2. ¿Quién viene a las diez?

   _____

3. ¿Quién viene a las once menos cuarto?

   _____

4. ¿Quién viene a las once y media?

   _____

5. ¿Quién viene a las doce?

   _____

6. ¿Quién viene a la una?

   _____

7. ¿Quién viene a las dos y media?

   _____

8. ¿Quién viene a las tres y media?

   _____

realidades.com

• Web Code: jcd-0513

Realidades **B**

Capítulo 5B

Nombre _____

Fecha _____

Hora _____

Core Practice **5B–6**

Una carta para mamá

Read the following letter from Rosaura to her mom in Spain. Write the form of **ser** or **estar** that best completes each sentence.

Querida mamá:

¡Aquí _____ en Chicago! Chicago _____ una gran ciudad con muchas personas que _____ muy interesantes. La comida _____ fantástica. La especialidad _____ la pizza. ¡Qué rica!

Vivo con una familia muy simpática. Tienen un hijo que siempre _____ contento y una hija que _____ muy estudiosa. ¡_____ las nueve de la noche y ella _____ en la biblioteca!

Los chicos de la escuela también _____ estudiosos, pero no muy serios. Mis compañeros y yo _____ muy buenos amigos y _____ juntos todos los fines de semana. Una amiga, Vera, _____ boliviana y _____ divertidísima. Vera y yo _____ en la misma clase de biología.

Bueno, mamá, _____ muy tarde. Mañana voy a _____ muy ocupada y necesito dormir. Pero sabes ahora que todo _____ bien aquí y que yo _____ contenta. Besos para ti y para papá.

Un abrazo,

Rosaura

Realidades Ⓑ

Capítulo 5B

Nombre _____

Fecha _____

Hora _____

Core Practice **5B–7**

¿Qué van a comer?

The Vázquez family is getting ready to order dinner in a restaurant. Look at the pictures to get an idea of the person's needs. Answer the questions below using vocabulary that would most logically go in each situation.

1.

¿Cómo está la Sra. Vázquez? _____

¿Qué debe pedir de plato principal? _____

¿De postre? _____ ¿Y para beber? _____

2.

¿Cómo están los chicos? _____

¿Qué deben pedir de plato principal? _____

¿De postre? _____ ¿Y para beber? _____

3.

¿Cómo está Elisita? _____

¿Qué debe pedir de plato principal? _____

¿De postre? _____ ¿Y para beber? _____

4.

¿Cómo está el Sr. Vázquez? _____

¿Qué debe pedir de plato principal? _____

¿De postre? _____ ¿Y para beber? _____

Realidades B

Capítulo 5B

Nombre _____

Fecha _____

Hora _____

Core Practice **5B–8**

Repaso

Across _____

6. *blond;* el pelo ____

7. Shaquille O'Neal es ____ .

8. Uds. ____ cansados.

12. Paquito no es viejo. Es ____ .

13. ¡Camarero, la ____ por favor!

15.

16. Mi abuela tiene el pelo ____ .

17. Ella tiene 88 años. Es ____ .

18. Necesito un cuchillo y un ____ para comer el bistec.

19. sal y ____

21. Necesito un té. Tengo ____ .

Down _____

1. *red-haired (m.)*

2. El Sr. López es un ____ .

3. *napkin*

4. Nosotros ____ bajos.

5. *good-looking (f.)*

9. ____ el pelo ____

10. ¿Qué quieres de ____? El flan.

11. Quiero un té helado. Tengo ____ .

13. no largo

14.

18. Quiero una ____ de café.

19. el plato ____

20. La Sra. Miranda es una ____ .

Realidades Ⓑ

Capítulo 5B

Nombre _____

Fecha _____

Hora _____

Core Practice **5B–9**

Organizer

I. Vocabulary

To describe people

_____
_____
_____
_____
_____
_____
_____

Words to order food and beverages

_____
_____
_____

Things at a restaurant

_____
_____
_____
_____
_____

Words to describe how you're feeling

_____
_____
_____

II. Grammar

1. The forms of **venir** are: _____ _____

   _____ _____

   _____ _____

2. For physical and personality descriptions, and to tell what time it is, use the verb

   _____. To talk about location and physical and emotional states,

   use the verb _____.

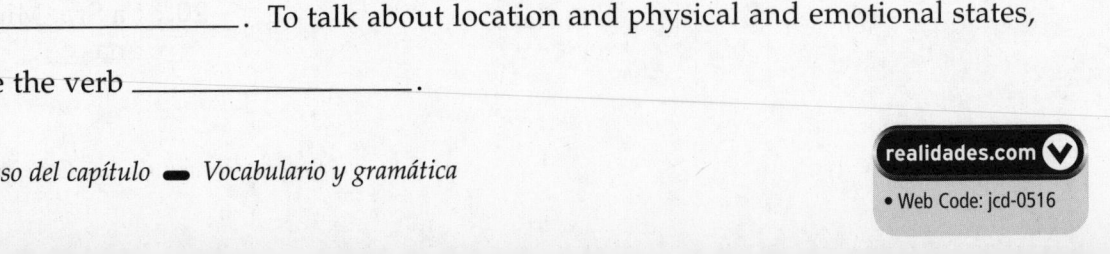

realidades.com Ⓥ
• Web Code: jcd-0516

Realidades B

Capítulo 6A

Nombre _____

Hora _____

Fecha _____

Core Practice **6A–1**

Un dormitorio nuevo para mí

Ignacio is moving into his sister's room when she goes away to college. His parents have told him that he can bring anything into his new room that he can carry by himself. Make a list of eight things that he would definitely be able to bring with him, and five things that he definitely wouldn't be able to bring. Use the examples given to help you.

Traer conmigo

El lector DVD

_____

_____

_____

_____

_____

_____

_____

No traer conmigo

La pared

_____

_____

_____

_____

Realidades Ⓑ

Capítulo 6A

Nombre _____

Fecha _____

Hora _____

Core Practice **6A-2**

Muchos colores

Write the names of the color or colors that you associate with the following things. Don't forget to make the colors agree in gender and number.

1. el jugo de naranja _____

2. la limonada _____

3. el 14 de febrero _____

4. el 25 de diciembre _____

5. el sol _____

6. la nieve _____

7. unas zanahorias _____

8. la bandera de los Estados Unidos _____

9. un tomate _____

10. la piscina _____

11. la noche _____

12. el Día de San Patricio _____

• Web Code: jcd-0601

Realidades **B**

Capítulo 6A

Nombre _____

Fecha _____

Hora _____

Core Practice **6A–3**

La experiencia nueva

A. Read the letter that Gloria wrote to her friend in Spain about her host family in Chile.

Querida Sandra,

Lo paso muy bien aquí con la familia Quijano. Desde el primer día aquí, tengo mi propio dormitorio. Hay una cama, una mesita, una lámpara, un escritorio con una silla pequeña y un espejo. También hay una ventana con cortinas amarillas. La mejor cosa del cuarto es la lámpara. Es roja, negra y marrón y es muy artística. Creo que es la lámpara más bonita del mundo.

El cuarto también es bonito. Las paredes son moradas. Sólo quiero mi equipo de sonido y mis discos compactos.

Abrazos,

Gloria

B. Now, answer these questions in complete sentences.

1. ¿A Gloria le gusta la familia?

_____

2. ¿Comparte Gloria el dormitorio con otro estudiante?

_____

3. ¿De qué color son las paredes en el dormitorio de Gloria?

_____

4. ¿Tiene Gloria su equipo de sonido en su dormitorio?

_____

5. ¿Cómo es la lámpara en el dormitorio de Gloria? ¿A ella le gusta?

_____

6. ¿De qué color son las cortinas en el dormitorio de Gloria?

Realidades Ⓑ

Capítulo 6A

Nombre _____

Fecha _____

Hora _____

Core Practice **6A–4**

¿Dónde está todo?

Movers just finished putting everything into Marcela's new room. Help her locate everything by describing where the items are in the picture below. Follow the model.

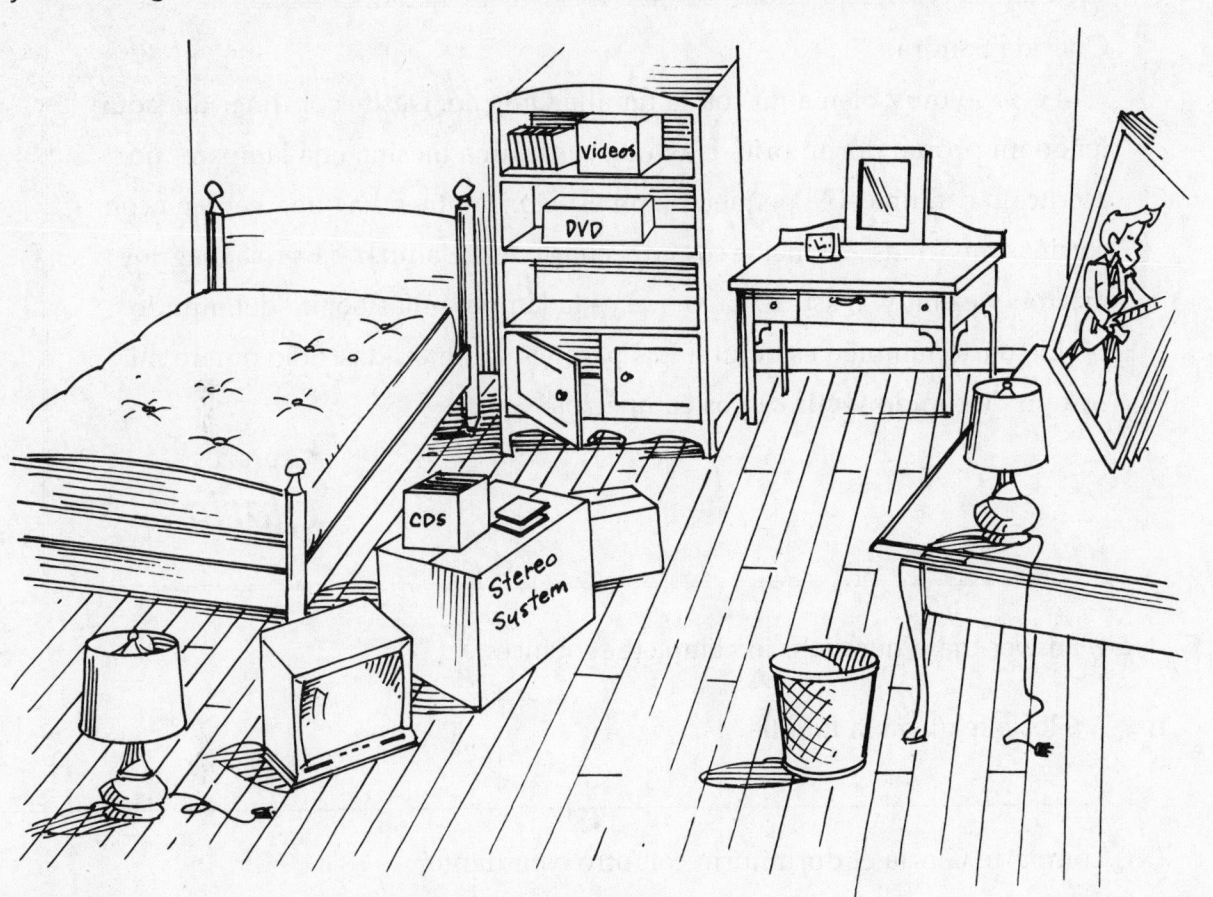

| **Modelo** | *Una lámpara está al lado del televisor.* |

_____

_____

_____

_____

_____

_____

_____

realidades.com ⓥ

• Web Code: jcd-0602

Realidades **B**

Capítulo 6A

Nombre

Fecha

Hora

Core Practice **6A–5**

Las comparaciones

Felipe and Mónica are brother and sister who are very different from each other. Using their pictures and the model to help you, write comparisons of the two siblings. Remember to make the adjectives agree in gender with the subject.

Modelo   Mónica / alto   *Mónica es más alta que Felipe.*

1. Felipe / serio _____

2. Mónica / sociable _____

3. Mónica / rubio _____

4. Felipe / estudioso _____

5. Felipe / alto _____

6. Mónica / viejo _____

7. Felipe / rubio _____

8. Felipe / joven _____

9. Mónica / serio _____

• Web Code: jcd-0603

Realidades B

Capítulo 6A

Nombre _____

Fecha _____

Hora _____

Core Practice **6A–6**

Los premios Óscar

The following chart rates movies according to certain categories. Four stars is the best rating, one star is the worst rating. Using the chart as a guide, write complete sentences comparing the three movies. Follow the model.

	Una tarde en agosto	*Mi vida*	*Siete meses en Lima*
Actores – talentosos	****	**	***
Fotografía – artística	****	*	***
Ropa – bonita	***	****	***
Director – creativo	****	***	**
Cuento – interesante	****	**	*

Modelo   actores / "Una tarde en agosto"

Los actores de "Una tarde en agosto" son los más talentosos.

1. fotografía / "Una tarde en agosto"

   _____

2. fotografía / "Mi vida"

   _____

3. director / "Una tarde en agosto"

   _____

4. actores / "Una tarde en agosto"

   _____

5. director / "Siete meses en Lima"

   _____

6. ropa / "Mi vida"

   _____

7. cuento / "Siete meses en Lima"

   _____

8. actores / "Mi vida"

   _____

9. cuento / "Una tarde en agosto"

   _____

Realidades **B**

Capítulo 6A

Nombre _____

Hora _____

Fecha _____

Core Practice **6A–7**

Las mini-conversaciones

A. Fill in the rest of these conjugations.

	DORMIR	**PODER**
yo		
tú		*puedes*
él, ella, Ud.	*duerme*	
nosotros		
vosotros	*dormís*	*podéis*
ellos, ellas, Uds.		

B. Write the correct forms of either **dormir** or **poder** in the blanks to complete the mini-conversations below.

1. — ¿Quieres ir al cine?

— No _____ . Tengo que trabajar.

2. — ¿Cuántas horas _____ cada noche?

— Generalmente, ocho horas.

3. — ¿Uds. _____ venir a nuestra fiesta?

— Sí. ¿A qué hora es?

4. — Nosotros no _____ trabajar hoy.

— Está bien. Van a trabajar mañana.

5. — Cuando ellas van de cámping, ¿dónde _____?

— Pues, en sus sacos de dormir, por supuesto.

6. — ¿Qué haces a las once y media de la noche?

— ¡Yo _____!

7. — ¿_____ (tú) hablar con tu abuela por teléfono?

— No, no _____ porque estoy ocupado.

8. — ¿Qué hace una chica cansada?

— _____ mucho.

Realidades **B**

Capítulo 6A

Nombre _____

Fecha _____

Hora _____

Core Practice **6A–8**

Repaso

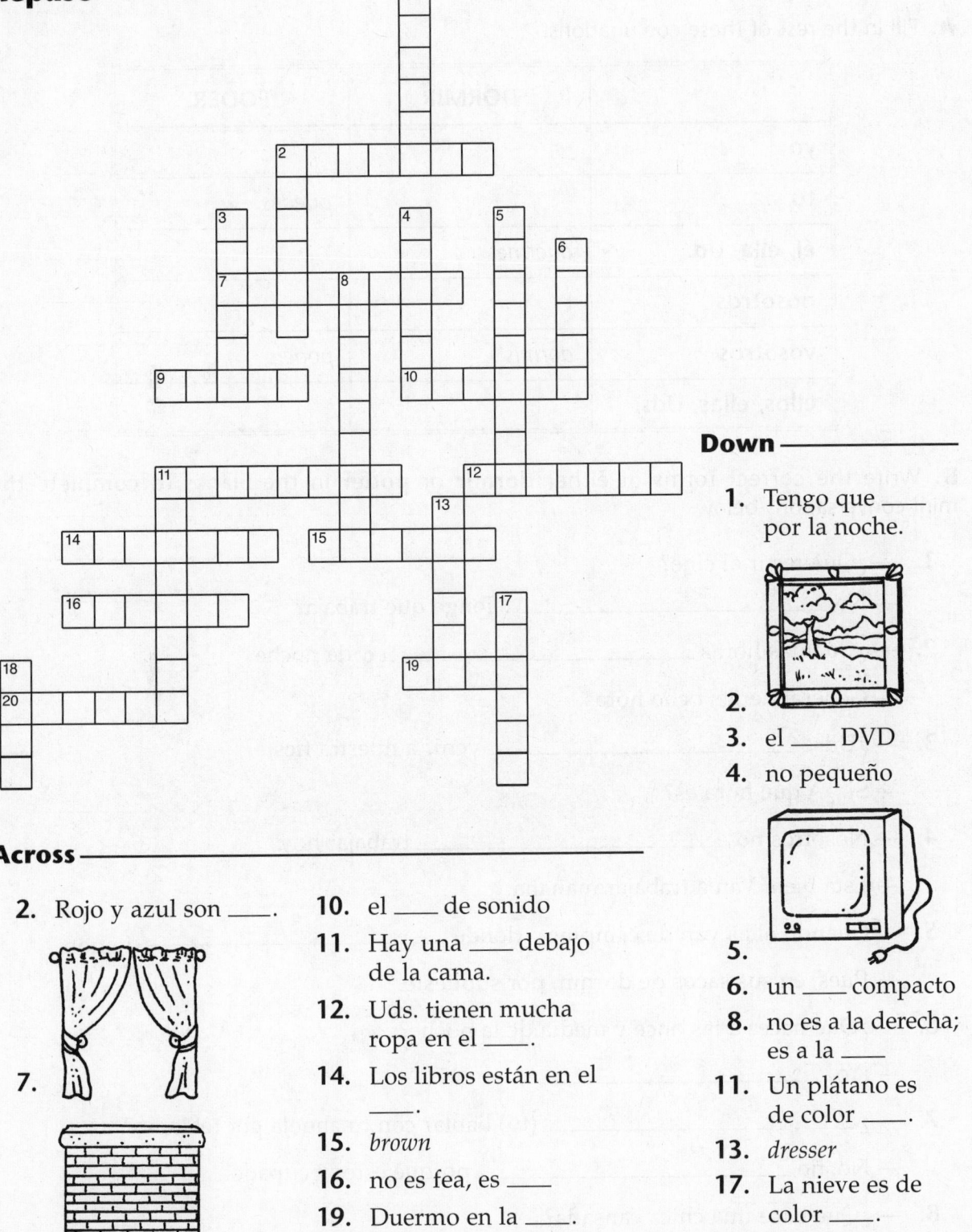

Down

1. Tengo que ____ por la noche.
2.
3. el ____ DVD
4. no pequeño
5.
6. un ____ compacto
8. no es a la derecha; es a la ____
11. Un plátano es de color ____.
13. *dresser*
17. La nieve es de color ____.
18. no mejor

Across

2. Rojo y azul son ____.
7.
9.
10. el ____ de sonido
11. Hay una ____ debajo de la cama.
12. Uds. tienen mucha ropa en el ____.
14. Los libros están en el ____.
15. *brown*
16. no es fea, es ____
19. Duermo en la ____.
20. *mirror*

Organizer

I. Vocabulary

To talk about things in a bedroom

_____

_____

_____

_____

_____

_____

Words to describe things

_____

_____

_____

_____

Electronic equipment

_____

_____

_____

_____

Words to talk about colors

_____

_____

_____

_____

II. Grammar

1. To compare peoples' ages, use either _____ + **que** or _____ + **que**. To say that something is "better than" use _____ + **que**; to say that something is "worse than" use _____ + **que**.

2. To say that something is the "best" or "worst" use the following construction: article + _____ / _____ + noun. To say "most" or "least" the construction is article + noun + _____ / _____ + adjective.

3. The forms of **poder** are: The forms of **dormir** are:

   _____ _____   _____ _____

   _____ _____   _____ _____

   _____ _____   _____ _____

Realidades B

Capítulo 6B

Nombre _____

Fecha _____

Hora _____

Core Practice **6B–1**

Los cuartos

The Suárez family has just moved into a new house. Tell what rooms are on each floor of the house.

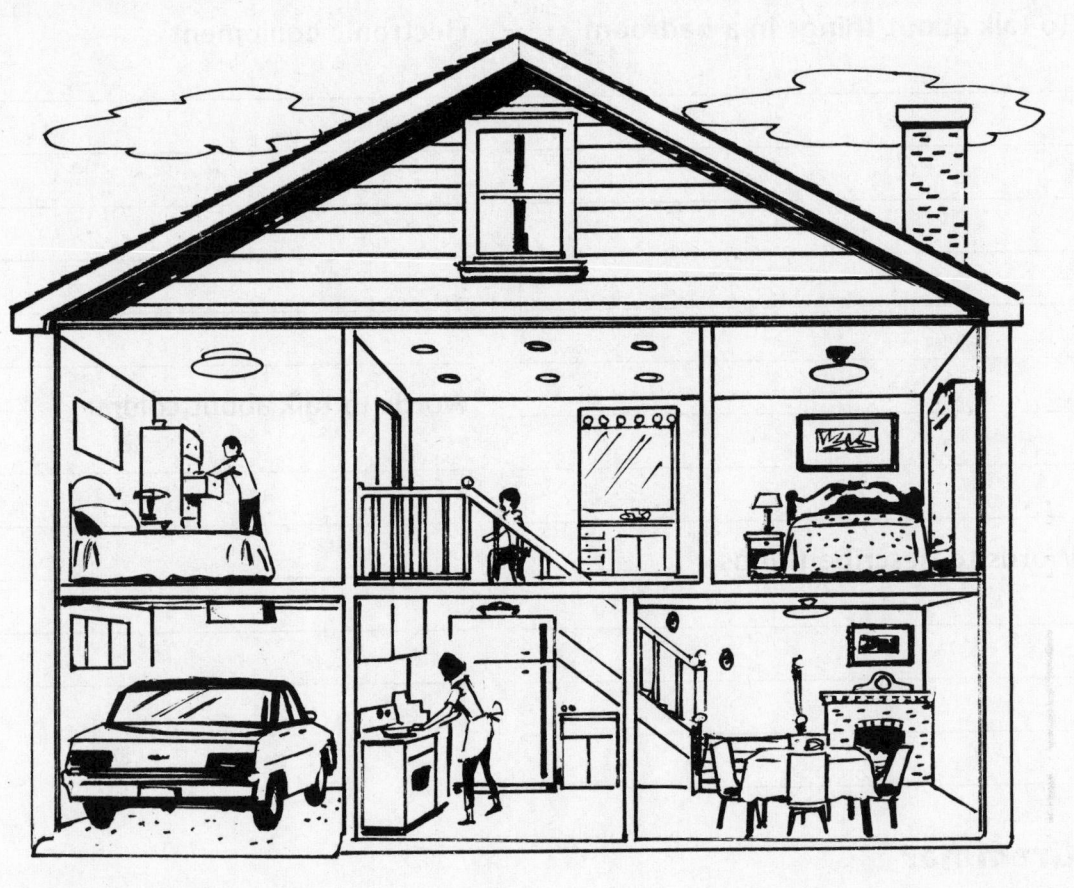

En la planta baja hay: _____

_____

_____

_____

En el primer piso hay: _____

_____

_____

_____

_____

realidades.com

• Web Code: jcd-0611

Realidades B

Capítulo 6B

Nombre _____

Fecha _____

Hora _____

Core Practice **6B–2**

Los quehaceres

Each person below has been given a location from which to do his or her chores. In the spaces provided, list at least two chores each person could logically be doing. Follow the model.

Modelo Alberto y Antonio están en el garaje.

lavan el coche

sacan la basura

limpian el garaje

1. Dolores está en el baño.

_____

_____

2. Eugenio está en el dormitorio.

_____

_____

3. Carolina y Catarina están en la sala.

_____

_____

4. Vladimir está en el comedor.

_____

_____

5. Ana Gracia está en la cocina.

_____

_____

Realidades B

Capítulo 6B

Nombre _____

Fecha _____

Hora _____

Core Practice **6B–3**

La lista de quehaceres

Melisa's mom has left her a list of the things that she has to do before her relatives come over for a dinner party. Complete the list with the appropriate word or phrase. Follow the model.

Modelo ___*Arregla*___ tu cuarto.

1. _____ la mesa del comedor.

2. Tienes que _____ porque no tienes ropa limpia.

3. _____ porque no tenemos platos limpios.

4. ¿Puedes _____? Hay demasiada basura.

5. _____ los platos en la cocina.

6. Necesitas _____ porque el coche está sucio.

7. Hay que _____ porque hay mucho polvo en el primer piso.

8. _____ las camas.

9. ¿Puedes _____ por las alfombras?

10. El baño no está limpio. Necesitas _____.

11. _____ de comer al perro.

12. Si tienes tiempo, _____ todos los quehaceres.

realidades.com

• Web Code: jcd-0612

Realidades B

Capítulo 6B

Nombre _____

Fecha _____

Hora _____

Core Practice **6B–4**

No es correcto

The following statements do not make sense. Rewrite the sentences by replacing the underlined words or phrases with words or phrases that make sense. Follow the model.

Modelo Nunca <u>haces</u> en casa cuando tienes quehaceres.
Nunca ayudas en casa cuando tienes quehaceres .

1. Tengo que <u>dar</u> la aspiradora por las alfombras.

   _____ .

2. El cuarto está <u>limpio</u>. Voy a limpiarlo.

   _____ .

3. Papá va a lavar platos en <u>el dormitorio</u>.

   _____ .

4. No te <u>recibo</u> dinero porque no estás haciendo nada.

   _____ .

5. <u>¡Haz la cama!</u> Vamos a comer.

   _____ .

6. Mamá lava <u>el coche</u> en la cocina.

   _____ .

7. ¿Cuáles son los <u>dinero</u> que tienes que hacer?

   _____ .

8. Doy <u>dinero</u> al perro todos los días.

   _____ .

9. Debes cortar <u>el polvo</u>, está bastante largo.

   _____ .

10. Ernesto quita <u>el coche</u> de la sala.

    _____ .

11. Las hermanas <u>cocinan</u> la basura por la noche.

    _____ .

Realidades B

Capítulo 6B

Nombre _____

Fecha _____

Hora _____

Core Practice **6B–5**

Los mandatos

A. Write the affirmative **tú** command forms of the following verbs in the spaces provided.

1. correr _____

2. poner _____

3. hacer _____

4. comer _____

5. hablar _____

6. leer _____

7. limpiar _____

8. ver _____

9. cortar _____

10. abrir _____

11. escribir _____

B. Now, write the chore your parents might tell you to do in each of the following situations. Follow the model.

Modelo Tu dormitorio no está limpio.   *Arregla tu dormitorio* .

1. El coche está sucio. _____ .

2. El perro tiene hambre. _____ .

3. No hay platos limpios. _____ .

4. Hay mucha basura en el garaje. _____ .

5. La camisa blanca ahora es gris. _____ .

6. Necesitamos cenar. _____ .

7. El baño no está limpio. _____ .

8. Hay mucho polvo en la sala. _____ .

realidades.com

• Web Code: jcd-0613

Nombre ______ Hora ______

Fecha ______

¿Qué están haciendo?

The Duarte family is getting ready for a barbecue. Look at the picture, then write what each of the family members is doing. Follow the model.

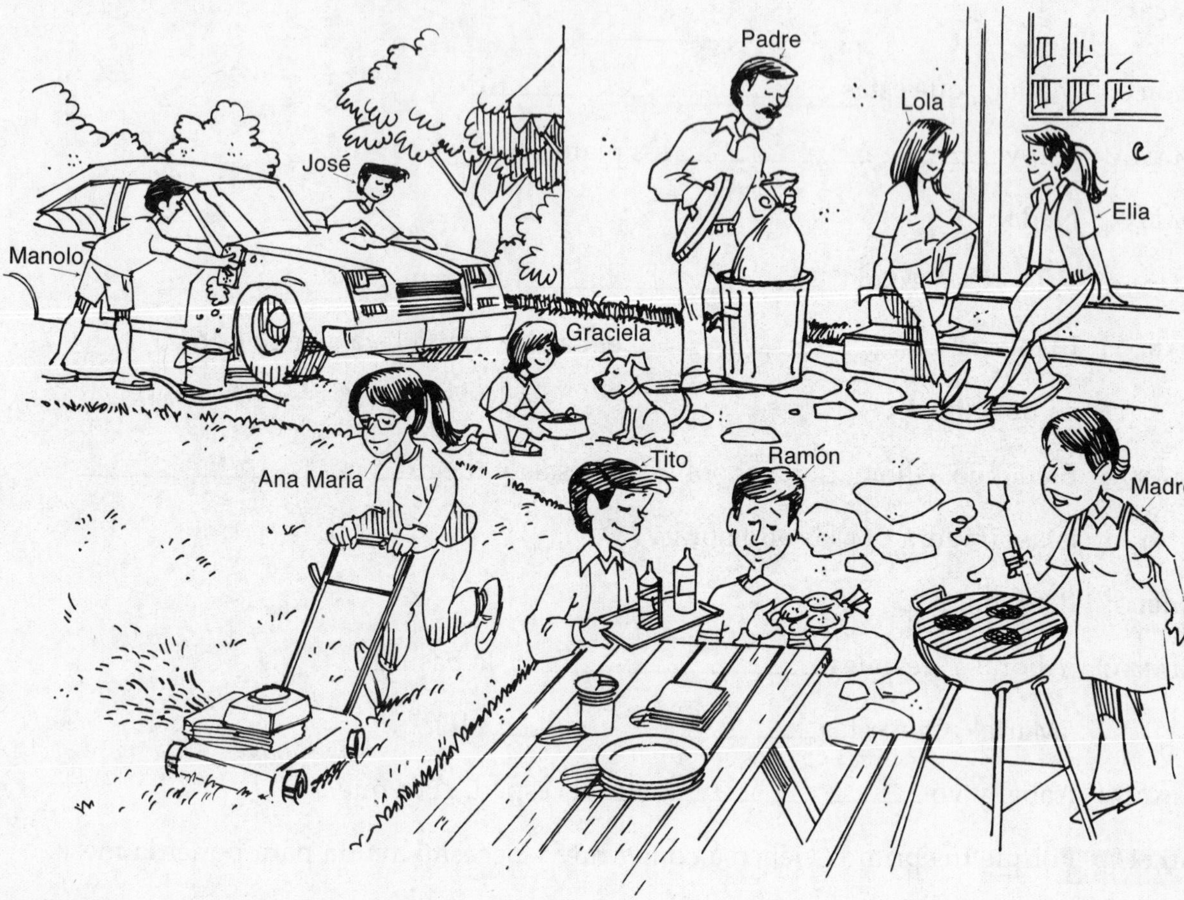

Modelo La madre *está cocinando las hamburguesas* ______.

1. Manolo y José ______.
2. Ana María ______.
3. El padre ______.
4. Tito y Ramón ______.
5. Graciela ______.
6. Lola y Elia ______.
7. Todos ______.

Realidades B

Capítulo 6B

Nombre _____

Fecha _____

Hora _____

Core Practice **6B–7**

Mucho trabajo

The Escobar family is getting ready to have guests over. Fill in the blanks in their conversation below with the appropriate form of the following verbs: **cortar, ayudar, hacer, lavar, pasar, sacar.**

PABLO: Mamá, ¿qué estás _____ tú?

MAMÁ: Estoy _____ los platos, hijo. ¿Y tú?

PABLO: Nada.

MAMÁ: Vale. ¿Qué están _____ tus hermanos?

PABLO: Juan está _____ el baño y Marta está arreglando

su dormitorio.

MAMÁ: Bien, hijo. Ahora, quita el polvo de la sala y luego _____

la aspiradora por las alfombras.

PABLO: Pero, mamá …

MAMÁ: ¡Ahora! Y después _____ la basura …

¡María! ¿Qué estás _____ , hija?

MARÍA: Isabel y yo _____ el césped. ¿Por qué?

MAMÁ: Porque tus primos vienen a comer hoy y necesito ayuda para poner la mesa.

MARÍA: ¿Por qué no te está _____ papá?

MAMÁ: Papá, cariño, ¿dónde estás?

PAPÁ: Estoy en el garaje. Estoy _____ el coche.

MAMÁ: Ah, sí. Después, arregla nuestro cuarto y _____ tu ropa sucia.

PAPÁ: ¿Por qué?

MAMÁ: ¡Vienen tu hermano y su familia!

Realidades B

Capítulo 6B

Nombre _____

Hora _____

Fecha _____

Core Practice **6B-8**

Repaso

Across

4. cómo pasas al primer piso desde la planta baja; la ___

6. Yo ___ el baño.

9.

12. *to cook*

15. El hijo ___ la aspiradora cada fin de semana.

16.

___ el cuarto

17. La hija debe ___ los platos ahora.

18. un cuarto donde puedes poner el coche

20. cuarto donde come la familia; el ___

21. el piso más bajo de la casa

Down

1. el cuarto donde preparas la comida

2. Tengo que ___ la cama hoy.

3.

quitar el ___

5.

___ la basura

6. no cerca

7. Después de subir la escalera, estás en el ___ ___ .

8. Cuando entras en la casa, estás en la ___ ___ .

10. la oficina en la casa

11. ¿Quién va a ___ la mesa?

13. el cuarto donde ves la tele

14. el cuarto donde duermes

19. Mateo tiene que cortar el ___ .

21. no limpio

Realidades **B**

Capítulo 6B

Nombre _____

Hora _____

Fecha _____

Core Practice **6B–9**

Organizer

I. Vocabulary

Rooms of the house

_____

_____

_____

_____

_____

_____

_____

Outdoor chores

_____

_____

_____

Indoor household tasks

_____

_____

_____

_____

Floors of the house

_____

_____

_____

_____

II. Grammar

1. To talk about actions in progress, use the _____ tense. This is formed by adding -_____ to the roots of **-ar** verbs and -_____ to the roots of **-er** and **-ir** verbs.

2. **Tú** commands are the same as the _____ form of the _____ tense of verbs. But the **tú** command form of **poner** is _____ and of **hacer** is _____.

realidades.com
• Web Code: jcd-0616

Realidades Ⓑ

Capítulo 7A

Nombre _____

Fecha _____

Hora _____

Core Practice **7A–1**

En el escaparate (*store window*)

You are window shopping at a large department store and you decide to make a list of what they have and what everything costs. Using the picture, list seven items and their prices below. Follow the model.

| Modelo | *Los pantalones cuestan 35 dólares.* |

1. _____

2. _____

3. _____

4. _____

5. _____

6. _____

7. _____

Realidades B

Capítulo 7A

Nombre _____

Fecha _____

Hora _____

Core Practice **7A–2**

Tienda de la Gracia

A. Write the numbers below in Spanish.

1. 100 _____

2. 500 _____

3. 909 _____

4. 222 _____

5. 767 _____

6. 676 _____

7. 110 _____

8. 881 _____

B. Read the following statistics about the chain of stores **Tienda de la Gracia**. Then answer the questions that follow.

TIENDA DE LA GRACIA	
Tiendas	100
Trabajadores	324
Promedio diario (*daily average*) **de clientes**	760
Camisas	612
Pantalones	404

1. ¿Cuántas Tiendas de la Gracia hay?

_____

2. ¿Cuál es el promedio diario de clientes en cada tienda?

_____

3. ¿Cuántos trabajadores hay en las Tiendas de la Gracia?

_____

4. ¿Cuántos pantalones hay en cada tienda?

_____

5. ¿Y camisas?

_____

En el centro comercial

Tatiana and Mariana are in the local mall. Write the words that most logically complete their conversation as they go from store to store.

TATIANA: Vamos a esta tienda de ropa. Aquí tienen _____ elegante.

MARIANA: Bien. ¿Qué _____ comprar?

TATIANA: Necesito un vestido para la fiesta de mi primo.

DEPENDIENTA: ¿En qué puedo _____, señorita?

TATIANA: _____ un vestido elegante.

DEPENDIENTA: ¿Va Ud. a _____ el vestido a una fiesta o un baile formal?

TATIANA: A una fiesta. Me gusta este vestido.

MARIANA: ¿Cómo te _____?

TATIANA: ¡Me queda fantástico! Quiero comprarlo.

MARIANA: Vamos a otra tienda. Necesito _____ unos zapatos nuevos.

Vamos a esa tienda, tienen buenos precios allí.

TATIANA: Mira estos zapatos aquí.

MARIANA: ¿Cuánto cuestan?

TATIANA: Trescientos dólares. ¿Es un buen _____?

MARIANA: Sí. Y me quedan _____. Voy a comprar estos zapatos.

TATIANA: Bien. Pasamos a otra tienda.

MARIANA: La tienda de música está a la derecha. ¿Entramos?

TATIANA: Sí, ¡ _____!

Realidades **B**

Capítulo 7A

Nombre _____

Fecha _____

Hora _____

Core Practice **7A–4**

¿Qué llevan?

In complete sentences, describe two articles of clothing that each of the people below is wearing.

Pedro

A. _____

_____

B. _____

1. _____

Las hermanas Guzmán

A. _____

_____

B. _____

2. _____

La profesora Jones

A. _____

_____

B. _____

3. _____

El Dr. Cambambia

A. _____

_____

B. _____

4. _____

Anita

A. _____

_____

B. _____

5. _____

• Web Code: jcd-0702

Realidades **B**

Capítulo 7A

Nombre _____

Fecha _____

Hora _____

Core Practice **7A–5**

Algunos verbos nuevos

A. Fill in the chart below with the forms of the stem-changing verbs indicated.

	PENSAR	QUERER	PREFERIR
yo	*pienso*		
tú			*prefieres*
él, ella, Ud.		*quiere*	
nosotros			*preferimos*
vosotros	*pensáis*	*queréis*	*preferís*
ellos, ellas, Uds.		*quieren*	

B. Now, complete each sentence below by choosing the correct form of the verb **pensar**, **querer**, or **preferir**.

1. ¿ _____ (tú) la camisa roja o la camisa azul?

2. Nosotros _____ comprar un suéter nuevo.

3. Ellas _____ ir de compras hoy.

4. Vivian _____ llevar ropa elegante.

5. ¿Uds. _____ trabajar en la tienda de Mónica?

6. Yo _____ comprar los zapatos ahora.

7. Mis amigos y yo _____ jugar al fútbol cuando llueve.

8. Eduardo _____ ir a la fiesta con Brenda.

9. ¿Qué _____ (tú) hacer después de la escuela?

10. Marcelo y Claudio _____ ir al gimnasio después de la escuela.

11. Yo _____ buscar una bicicleta nueva.

12. ¿Tomás va a la tienda o _____ quedarse en casa?

Manos a la obra ▬ *Gramática y vocabulario en uso* **41**

Realidades Ⓑ

Capítulo 7A

Nombre _____

Hora _____

Fecha _____

Core Practice **7A–6**

¿Cuál prefieres?

A. Fill in the chart below with the singular and plural, masculine and feminine forms of the demonstrative adjectives.

este		estos	
	esa		esas

B. Complete the following questions about the clothing items pictured by writing in the appropriate demonstrative adjectives from the chart above. Then answer the questions by saying that you prefer the item indicated by the arrow.

1. — ¿Prefieres _____ camisa o _____ suéter?

— _____

2. — ¿Prefieres _____ pantalones cortos o _____ jeans?

— _____

3. — ¿Te gustan más _____ sudaderas aquí o _____ suéteres?

— _____

— _____

4. — ¿Te gusta más _____ vestido o _____ falda?

— _____

— _____

5. — ¿Quieres _____ zapatos negros o _____ botas negras?

— _____

6. — ¿Prefieres _____ chaqueta o _____ abrigo?

— _____

Realidades Ⓑ

Capítulo 7A

Nombre _____

Hora _____

Fecha _____

Core Practice **7A–7**

¿Quién?

Two sales associates are discussing some of the clients in their busy store. Fill in the blanks with the appropriate demonstrative adjectives based on the picture.

CELIA: ¿Qué hace _____ mujer allá?

YOLANDA: Pues, está mirando las botas, pero no quiere pagar mucho.

CELIA: ¿Qué quieren _____ mujeres aquí?

YOLANDA: Piensan comprar unos calcetines.

CELIA: ¿Y _____ hombre solo allí?

YOLANDA: ¿_____ hombre? Prefiere mirar los pantalones.

CELIA: A la derecha de él hay unos niños, ¿no? ¿Qué hacen _____ niños?

YOLANDA: Pues, _____ niños quieren unos suéteres nuevos.

CELIA: Oye, ¿ves a _____ hombres al lado de la puerta?

YOLANDA: Sí, piensan comprar _____ abrigos. ¿Por qué?

CELIA: Pues, son muy guapos, ¿no?

YOLANDA: Ah, sí. Creo que necesitan ayuda.

CELIA: ¡Hasta luego!

Realidades B

Capítulo 7A

Nombre _____

Fecha _____

Hora _____

Core Practice **7A–8**

Repaso

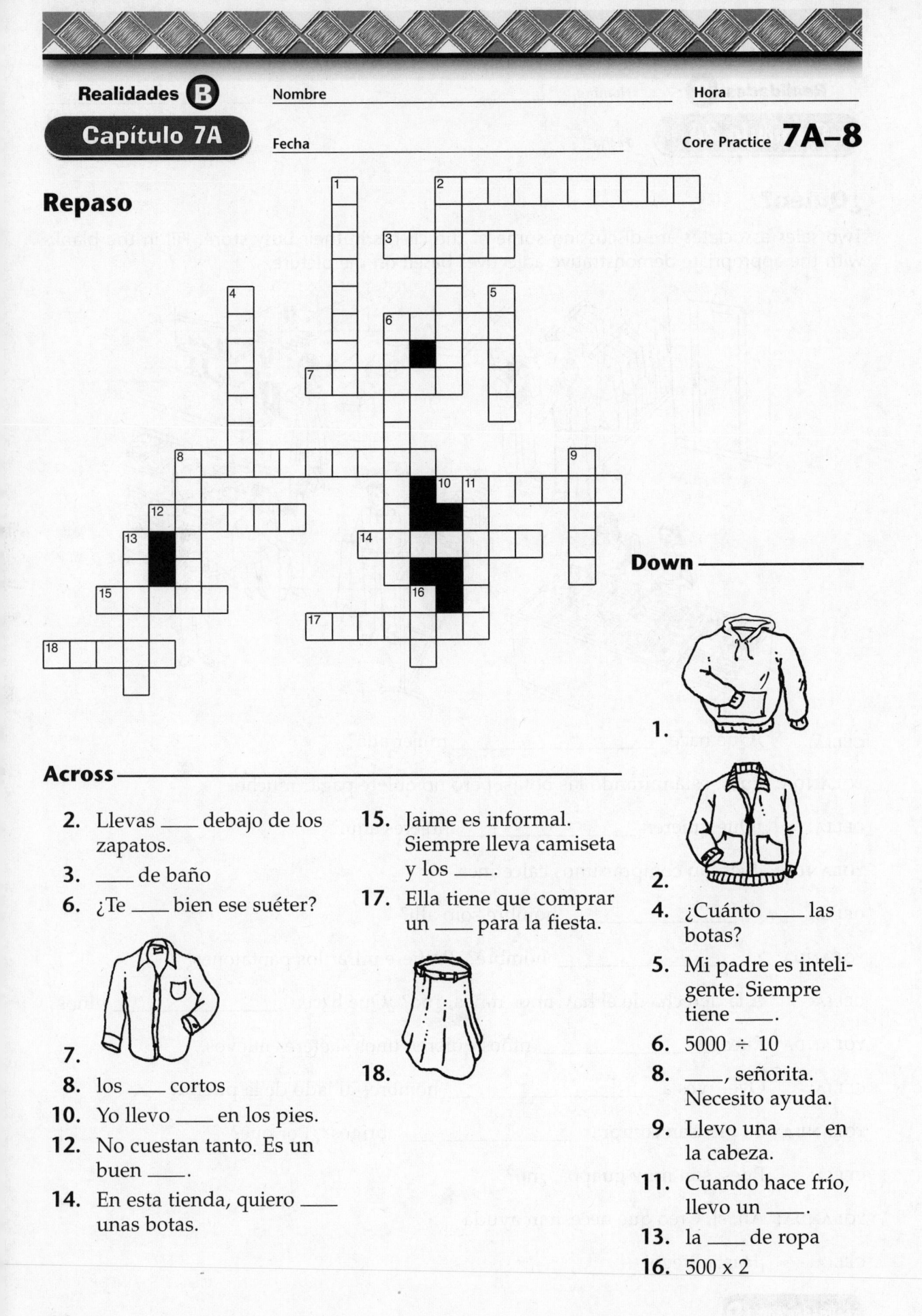

Across

2. Llevas ____ debajo de los zapatos.

3. ____ de baño

6. ¿Te ____ bien ese suéter?

7.

8. los ____ cortos

10. Yo llevo ____ en los pies.

12. No cuestan tanto. Es un buen ____.

14. En esta tienda, quiero ____ unas botas.

15. Jaime es informal. Siempre lleva camiseta y los ____.

17. Ella tiene que comprar un ____ para la fiesta.

18.

Down

1.

2.

4. ¿Cuánto ____ las botas?

5. Mi padre es inteligente. Siempre tiene ____.

6. 5000 ÷ 10

8. ____, señorita. Necesito ayuda.

9. Llevo una ____ en la cabeza.

11. Cuando hace frío, llevo un ____.

13. la ____ de ropa

16. 500 x 2

Realidades **B**

Capítulo 7A

Nombre _____

Fecha _____

Hora _____

Core Practice **7A–9**

Organizer

I. Vocabulary

Clothing for warm weather

_____

_____

_____

_____

Clothing for cold weather

_____

_____

_____

_____

_____

Other words to talk about clothing

_____

_____

_____

Numbers in the hundreds

_____

_____

_____

_____

_____

_____

II. Grammar

1. The forms of the verb **pensar** are: _____ _____

   _____ _____

   _____ _____

   The forms of the verb **querer** are: _____ _____

   _____ _____

   _____ _____

   The forms of the verb **preferir** are: _____ _____

   _____ _____

   _____ _____

2. To refer to something close, use _____ / _____ , _____ / _____ ; to refer to something further away, use _____ / _____ , _____ / _____ .

Realidades B

Capítulo 7B

Nombre _____

Fecha _____

Hora _____

Core Practice **7B–1**

Los regalos

Marcela is writing a list of gifts she wants to buy for her family. Help her by writing the names of the items suggested by the pictures in the blanks provided.

1. Para mi novio:

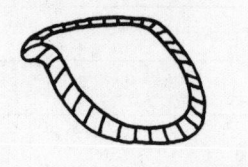   

_____ _____ _____ _____

2. Para mi mejor amiga:

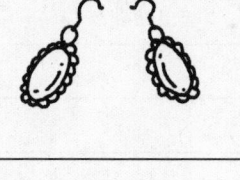 

_____ _____

3. Para mi hermana:

   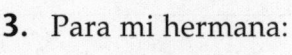

_____ _____ _____ _____

4. Para mi padre:

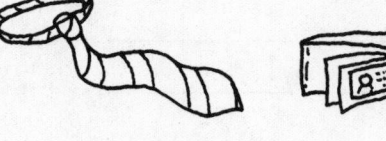 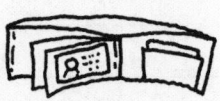 

_____ _____ _____

5. Para mi madre:

  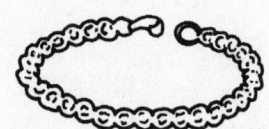

_____ _____ _____

realidades.com ⌄
• Web Code: jcd-0711

Realidades **B**

Capítulo 7B

Nombre _____

Fecha _____

Hora _____

Core Practice **7B–2**

¡Tantas tiendas!

Write the names of the items pictured in the first blank, and where each person would find the items in the second blank.

1. Yo busco _____

   en una _____.

2. Germán busca _____

   en una _____.

3. Tú buscas _____

   en la _____.

4. Mi hermano busca _____

   en la _____.

5. Bárbara busca _____

   en un _____.

6. Buscamos _____

   en la _____.

7. Esteban y Luis buscan un _____

   en la _____.

8. Susana y Paulina buscan _____

   en una _____.

9. — ¿En dónde puedo comprar _____?

   — En un _____.

Realidades B

Capítulo 7B

Nombre _____

Fecha _____

Hora _____

Core Practice **7B–3**

¿El regalo perfecto?

Valentine's Day is coming and Pepe and Laura are deciding what gifts to give each other.

A. Read the conversations below.

(*En una tienda de descuentos*)

PEPE: Necesito comprar un regalo para mi novia.

DEPENDIENTE: ¿Qué piensa comprar?

PEPE: No sé. Tiene que ser algo barato porque no tengo mucho dinero.

DEPENDIENTE: Pero, ¿no quiere un anillo bonito o un collar elegante para su novia?

PEPE: No. Es demasiado.

DEPENDIENTE: Puede comprar un reloj pulsera que no cuesta tanto.

PEPE: Oiga, el mes pasado compré software nuevo para mi computadora, para poder jugar videojuegos en la Red. ¡Pagué unos 90 dólares!

DEPENDIENTE: Entonces quiere este llavero de veinte dólares.

PEPE: ¡Genial!

(*En un almacén*)

LAURA: Quiero el regalo perfecto para mi novio.

DEPENDIENTA: ¿Él trabaja? ¿Quizás una corbata bonita?

LAURA: Estoy pensando en un regalo más romántico . . .

DEPENDIENTA: ¿Unos guantes para las noches de frío?

LAURA: No creo. Él nunca tiene frío. ¿Ud. tiene algo romántico?

DEPENDIENTA: ¡Mire! ¿Qué piensa de este anillo de cincuenta dólares?

LAURA: ¡Perfecto! Quiero uno, por favor.

B. Answer the questions about the dialogues in complete sentences.

1. ¿A qué tienda va Pepe? _____

   ¿Qué busca allí? ¿Por qué? _____

   _____

2. ¿Qué quiere venderle el dependiente? ¿Por qué Pepe no quiere comprarlos?

   _____

   _____

3. ¿Qué compra por fin Pepe? _____

4. ¿Qué quiere comprar Laura? _____

5. ¿Por qué Laura no quiere ni una corbata ni unos guantes? _____

   _____

6. ¿Qué va a comprar Laura? _____ ¿Es más

   caro o más barato que el regalo de Pepe? _____

• Web Code: jcd-0712

Realidades B

Capítulo 7B

Nombre _____

Fecha _____

Hora _____

Core Practice **7B–4**

Oraciones desordenadas

Put the scrambled sentences below into logical order.

1. compré / hace / lo / semana / una

_____

2. yo / por / ayer / unos / pagué / un / guantes / dólar

_____

3. lector / caro / DVD / un / es / muy / no

_____

4. joyas / en / venden / almacén / el

_____

5. pasada / la / compré / yo / semana / suéter / nuevo / un

_____

6. anoche / una / compré / computadora / yo / nueva

_____

7. pagaste / el / collar / cuánto / por

¿_____?

8. lo / año / el / tú / compraste / pasado

_____

9. joyas / por / venden / tienda / esta / veinte / en / dólares

_____

10. cuánto / por / el / pagaste / reloj

¿_____?

Realidades B

Capítulo 7B

Nombre _____

Fecha _____

Hora _____

Core Practice **7B–5**

Hablamos del pasado

A. Fill in the chart below with the preterite forms of the verbs indicated.

	COMPRAR	HABLAR	PREPARAR	USAR	MIRAR
yo	compré				
tú					miraste
él, ella, Ud.		habló			
nosotros				usamos	
vosotros	comprasteis	hablasteis	preparasteis	usasteis	mirasteis
ellos, ellas, Uds.			prepararon		

B. Fill in the blanks in the following postcard with the correct preterite forms of the verbs given.

¡Hola, mamá!

    ¿Cómo estás? Estoy muy bien aquí en Quito.
Primero, José y yo _____ (preparar) unos
sándwiches ricos y _____ (hablar) con su
mamá un poco. Después, decidimos ir al centro
comercial. José y su mamá _____ (mirar)
unas chaquetas en la tienda de Smith y yo
_____ (comprar) algunas cosas para la
semana.

    A las cinco, la mamá de José _____
(llamar) por teléfono al padre, y él _____
(regresar) del trabajo un poco después. Nosotros
_____ (cenar) y _____ (usar) la
computadora antes de dormir.

    ¿Y tú? ¿_____ (caminar) esta semana?
¿_____ (comprar) el regalo para el
cumpleaños de papi? Pues, nos vemos en una semana.
¡Mañana me voy a Lima!

          Un abrazo,

          Víctor

La Sra. Guiraldo
Vía Águila 1305
Col. Cuauhtémoc
06500 México, D.F.

realidades.com
• Web Code: jcd-0713

Realidades B

Capítulo 7B

Nombre _____

Fecha _____

Hora _____

Core Practice **7B–6**

Mini-conversaciones

A. Fill in the following charts with the preterite forms of the verbs given.

	PAGAR	BUSCAR	JUGAR	PRACTICAR	TOCAR
yo	*pagué*			*practiqué*	
tú			*jugaste*		
él, ella, Ud.		*buscó*			
nosotros					*tocamos*
vosotros	*pagasteis*	*buscasteis*	*jugasteis*	*practicasteis*	*tocasteis*
ellos, ellas, Uds.				*practicaron*	

B. Now, complete the mini-conversations below with preterite verb forms from the chart above.

1. — Juan, ¿cuánto _____ por tu suéter?

   — Yo _____ 25 dólares.

2. — ¿Qué hizo Marta anoche?

   — Ella _____ al fútbol con sus hermanos.

3. — Hija, ¿_____ el piano?

   — Sí, mamá. _____ por una hora.

4. — Busco un apartamento nuevo.

   — Yo _____ por un año antes de encontrar el apartamento perfecto.

5. — ¿Uds. _____ un instrumento en el pasado?

   — Sí, nosotros _____ el violín.

6. — ¿Marcos va a practicar el básquetbol hoy?

   — No, él _____ toda la semana pasada.

7. — ¿Con quién _____ (tú) al golf?

   — _____ con mis dos hermanos y con mi padre.

Realidades **B**

Capítulo 7B

Nombre _____

Fecha _____

Hora _____

Core Practice **7B–7**

Objeto directo

A. Rewrite the following sentences about shopping using direct object pronouns in place of the appropriate nouns.

1. Compré los zapatos. _____

2. ¿Tienes el vestido verde? _____

3. Escribo el cuento. _____

4. Mi mamá recibe el dinero. _____

5. Las mujeres llevan las faldas nuevas. _____

6. ¿Rosario va a comprar el regalo? _____

7. Las amigas compraron aretes nuevos. _____

8. Llevo los dos abrigos. _____

B. Ramona's mother is talking to her about their trip to the mall. Answer her questions using direct object pronouns. Follow the model.

Modelo ¿Llevas tu vestido nuevo a la escuela?

Sí, lo llevo mucho.

1. ¿Dónde vas a poner tu camisa nueva?

_____

2. ¿Compraste los zapatos azules?

_____

3. ¿Usas el reloj pulsera negro?

_____

4. ¿Cuándo vas a llevar tus guantes nuevos?

_____

5. ¿Tienes las camisetas nuevas?

_____

realidades.com
• Web Code: jcd-0715

Realidades Ⓑ

Capítulo 7B

Nombre _____

Fecha _____

Hora _____

Core Practice **7B–8**

Repaso

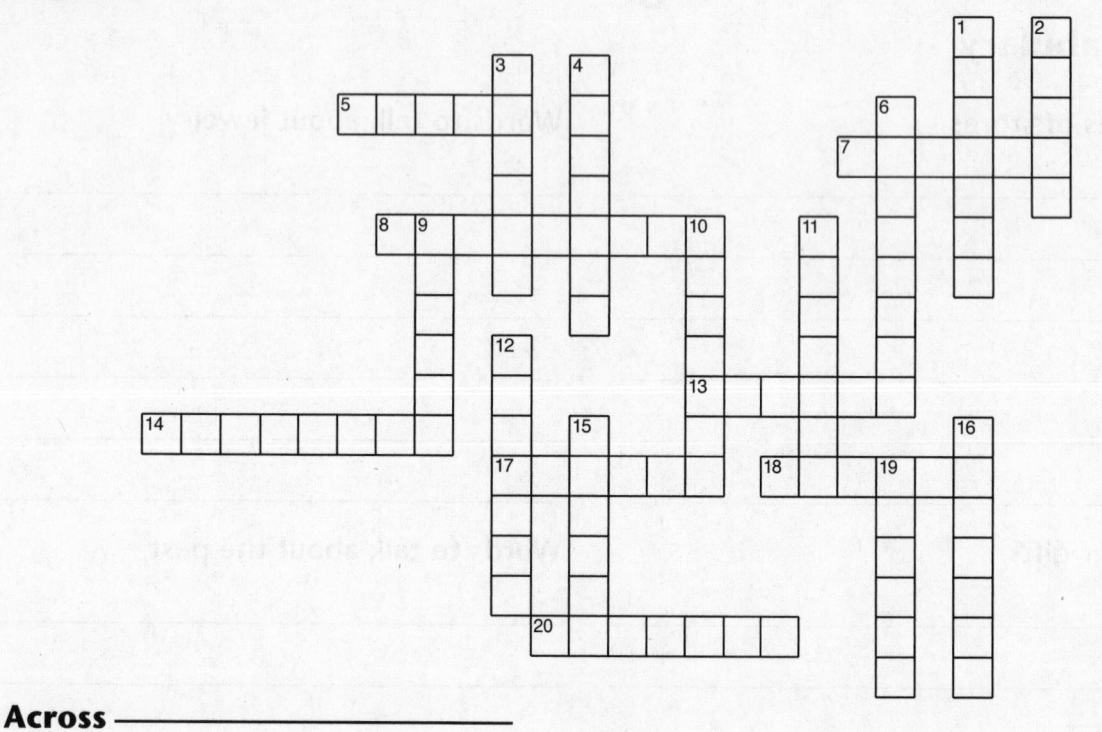

Across

5. donde las mujeres ponen las llaves, bolígrafos, etc.

7. la ___ de electrodomésticos

8. tienda donde venden zapatos

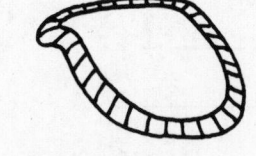

13.

14. los ___ de sol

17. Una tienda de ropa es donde ___ ropa.

18. no caro

20. tienda donde venden joyas

Down

1. Llevo los ___ durante el invierno porque tengo las manos frías.

2. Sancho quiere ___ las fotos de tu viaje.

3.

4. donde pones el dinero y a veces unas fotos; la ___

6. tienda donde venden libros

9. joya que llevas en las orejas

10. tienda donde venden de todo

11. tipo de reloj que llevas en el cuerpo; reloj ___

12. donde pones las llaves

15. joya que llevas en el dedo

16. Los hombres llevan una camisa con ___ al trabajo.

19. *last night*

Realidades B

Capítulo 7B

Nombre _____

Hora _____

Fecha _____

Core Practice **7B–9**

Organizer

I. Vocabulary

Types of stores

_____
_____
_____
_____
_____
_____

Words to talk about jewelry

_____
_____
_____
_____
_____
_____

Other gifts

_____
_____
_____
_____

Words to talk about the past

_____
_____
_____
_____
_____

II. Grammar

1. The preterite endings of **-ar** verbs are: -_____ -_____

   -_____ -_____

   -_____ -_____

   Now conjugate the verb **pasar** in the preterite: _____ _____

   _____ _____

   _____ _____

2. The preterite ending of the **yo** form of verbs ending with **-car** is -_____. For

   -gar verbs it is -_____.

3. The direct object pronouns are _____, _____, _____, and

   _____.

realidades.com
• Web Code: jcd-0717

Realidades Ⓑ

Capítulo 8A

Nombre _____

Fecha _____

Hora _____

Core Practice **8A–1**

¿Adónde van?

Complete the mini-conversations. Use the drawing to fill in the first blank and to give you a clue for the second blank. Follow the model.

Modelo

— ¿Viste el ___monumento___ nuevo de Cristóbal Colón?

— Sí, ¡es fantástico! Está enfrente del ___museo___.

1.

— Mamá, quiero ver _____.

— Sí, Marisol. Vamos al _____.

2.

— ¿Uds. van de vacaciones en _____ este verano?

— No, vamos a la _____.

3.

— ¿Vas a ver _____ hoy?

— Sí, mis padres y yo vamos al _____.

4.

— ¿Quieres _____ hoy?

— Sí, pero ¿en dónde? ¿En el _____?

5.

— ¿Dónde es el _____?

— Pues, en el _____, por supuesto.

6.

— ¿Cómo te gusta ir de _____?

— Siempre viajamos en _____.

• Web Code: jcd-0801

A primera vista ▬ *Vocabulario en contexto* **55**

Realidades B

Capítulo 8A

Nombre _____

Fecha _____

Hora _____

Core Practice **8A–2**

Asociaciones

A. Write the names of the places from your vocabulary that you associate with the following things or actions.

1. la historia, el arte ___ ___ ___ ⊖ ___ ___ ___ ___ ⊖ ___

2. las atracciones, los monos ___ ___ ___ ⊖ ___ ___ ___ ___ ___

3. pintar, dibujar, el arte ___ ___ ⊖ ___ ___

4. divertido, personas atrevidas, jugar ___ ___ ⊖ ___ ___ ___ ___   ___ ___

    ___ ___ ___ ⊖ ___ ___ ___ ⊖ ___

5. los deportes, un partido, ver ⊖ ___ ___ ___ ⊖ ___ ___

6. la obra, el actor ___ ⊖ ___ ___ ___ ___

7. el hotel, muchas personas ⊖ ___ ___ ___ ___ ___

8. pasear en bote, mucha agua ___ ___ ___ ⊖

B. Now, unscramble the circled letters to find a related word.

___ ___ ___ ___   ___ ___ ___ ___ ___ ___ ___ ___ ___

realidades.com
• Web Code: jcd-0801

Realidades Ⓑ

Capítulo 8A

Nombre _____

Fecha _____

Hora _____

Core Practice **8A-3**

¡Vamos al parque nacional!

The Carreras family went on vacation to Rocky Mountain National Park in Colorado. Read the postcard they sent to their friends back home and fill in the blanks with the words suggested by the pictures.

¡Saludos desde Colorado!

Llegamos al _____ el lunes pasado. Yo fui directamente

a la playa para _____ El _____

es precioso y ¡los _____ son enormes! El martes paseamos

en _____ por el lago y miramos los _____

_____. ¡Yo vi un oso en el bosque!

Para mañana tenemos muchos planes. Vamos a _____

por las montañas y por la noche vamos al _____ para ver

una obra musical.

Regresamos a la _____ el viernes. ¡Nos vemos

este fin de semana!

Abrazos,

Familia Carreras

Realidades B

Capítulo 8A

Nombre _____

Fecha _____

Hora _____

Core Practice **8A–4**

¿Qué te pasó?

A. Read the dialogue between Aníbal and Carmen about Aníbal's trip to the beach.

CARMEN: Dime, ¿fuiste a la playa con tus primos?

ANÍBAL: ¡Ay, amiga; fue un desastre! Salí muy temprano para pasar todo el día allí.

Durante el día tomamos el sol y buceamos en el mar.

CARMEN: ¿No fue un día tremendo para descansar y pasarlo bien con tus amigos?

ANÍBAL: Por dos horas, sí. Pero después de mucha lluvia, todo salió mal.

CARMEN: Lo siento. Va a hacer buen tiempo este sábado. . .

ANÍBAL: Bueno, tú y yo podemos salir de la ciudad.

CARMEN: ¡Genial!

B. Now, answer the questions in complete sentences.

1. ¿Adónde fue Aníbal? _____

_____

2. ¿Qué hizo allí? _____

3. ¿Con quién fue Aníbal? _____

4. ¿Qué tiempo va a hacer el sábado? _____

_____

5. ¿Qué van a hacer Aníbal y Carmen? _____

_____

realidades.com
• Web Code: jcd-0802

¿Qué hicieron?

A. Fill in the chart with the preterite forms of the verbs given.

	COMER	ESCRIBIR	CORRER	SALIR	VER	BEBER
yo	comí				vi	
tú			corriste	saliste	viste	bebiste
él, ella, Ud.				salió		bebió
nosotros		escribimos				
vosotros	comisteis	escribisteis	corristeis	salisteis	visteis	bebisteis
ellos/as, Uds.						

B. Now, complete the mini-conversations below by filling in the appropriate forms of one of the verbs from Part A.

1. — Pablo, ¿vas a correr hoy?

   — No, _____ ayer.

2. — ¿Elena _____ toda la leche?

   — Sí, toda.

3. — ¿Uds. salieron anoche?

   — Sí, _____ a las once.

4. — ¿_____ la nueva película de Almodóvar?

   — Sí, la vi anoche.

5. — ¡Qué buenos niños!

   — Sí, _____ todas las zanahorias.

6. — Juan, escribe la tarea.

   — Ya la _____ , mamá.

7. — ¿Uds. comieron en el hotel anoche?

   — No, _____ en el restaurante.

8. — ¿Quién va a correr en el maratón este año?

   — Todos, porque sólo dos personas _____ el año pasado.

9. — ¿Con quién saliste, Marta?

   — _____ con Toño.

10. — ¿El autor va a escribir un cuento nuevo?

    — No, él _____ uno el mes pasado.

Realidades B

Capítulo 8A

Nombre _____

Fecha _____

Hora _____

Core Practice **8A–6**

¿Adónde fueron?

Some friends are talking about where they went on vacation. Write where they went, using the pictures below to help you. Follow the model.

Modelo La familia Madrigal *fue al zoológico* _____.

1. Carlos _____.

2. Yo _____.

3. Lola y Tina _____.

4. Nosotros _____.

5. Elisa _____.

6. Tú _____.

7. Uds. _____.

realidades.com
• Web Code: jcd-0804

Realidades **B**

Capítulo 8A

Nombre _____

Fecha _____

Hora _____

Core Practice **8A–7**

¿Qué viste?

Alicia saw many things at the park yesterday. Use the drawing and the location clues to say whom or what she saw. Pay attention to the use of the personal **a** in your statements. Follow the model.

Modelo En el parque ayer, yo vi ___*a unos amigos*___ corriendo.

1. Yo vi _____ dándoles de comer a unos pájaros.

2. Yo vi _____ jugando al fútbol.

3. Yo vi _____ en la mesa.

4. En el lago, yo vi _____ paseando.

5. En el bote, yo vi _____ con una señorita.

6. En un árbol yo vi _____.

7. Al lado del árbol vi _____.

8. Debajo del árbol vi _____ con pelo largo.

9. En la playa vi _____.

Realidades B

Capítulo 8A

NOMBRE _____

FECHA _____

HORA _____

Core Practice **8A–8**

Repaso

Down ───────────────

1. Me gusta ___ en el sofá.
2. donde puedes pasear en bote; el ___
3. Yo quiero ___ la tele.
4. medio de transporte que va por el agua; el ___
5. un edificio con muchos cuadros; el ___
8. medio de transporte que usan los estudiantes para ir a la escuela; el ___
10. la ___ de teatro
12. *the train*; el ___
13. *the sea*; el ___
14. sinónimo de **vacaciones**; un ___

17.

20. Chicago es una ___ donde hace mucho viento.

22.

Across ───────────────

2. *place*; un ___
6. En el monumento, compramos ___.
7. el ___ de diversiones

9.

11. donde se juegan los partidos de fútbol; el ___
15. España es un ___ donde hablan español.
16. medio de transporte que va por el aire; el ___
18. pasear en ___
19. donde hay atracciones de animales; el ___
21. no tarde

Realidades Ⓑ

Capítulo 8A

Nombre _____

Hora _____

Fecha _____

Core Practice **8A–9**

Organizer

I. Vocabulary

Places to visit

_____

_____

_____

_____

Modes of transportation

_____

_____

_____

_____

Leisure activities

_____

_____

_____

_____

Phrases to discuss experiences

_____

_____

_____

_____

II. Grammar

1. The preterite endings of **-er** and **-ir** verbs are:

   yo   -_____   nosotros -_____

   tú   -_____   vosotros -_*isteis*_

   Ud. -_____   Uds.   -_____

2. The preterite forms of **ir** (and **ser**) are: _____ _____

   _____ _____

   _____ _____

3. _____ is inserted before the direct object of a sentence if the direct object is

   a person. This is called the _____.

Realidades B

Capítulo 8B

Nombre _____

Fecha _____

Hora _____

Core Practice **8B-1**

La comunidad

Your new friend in Costa Rica is showing you around her community. Label each place or point of interest in the picture with the appropriate word.

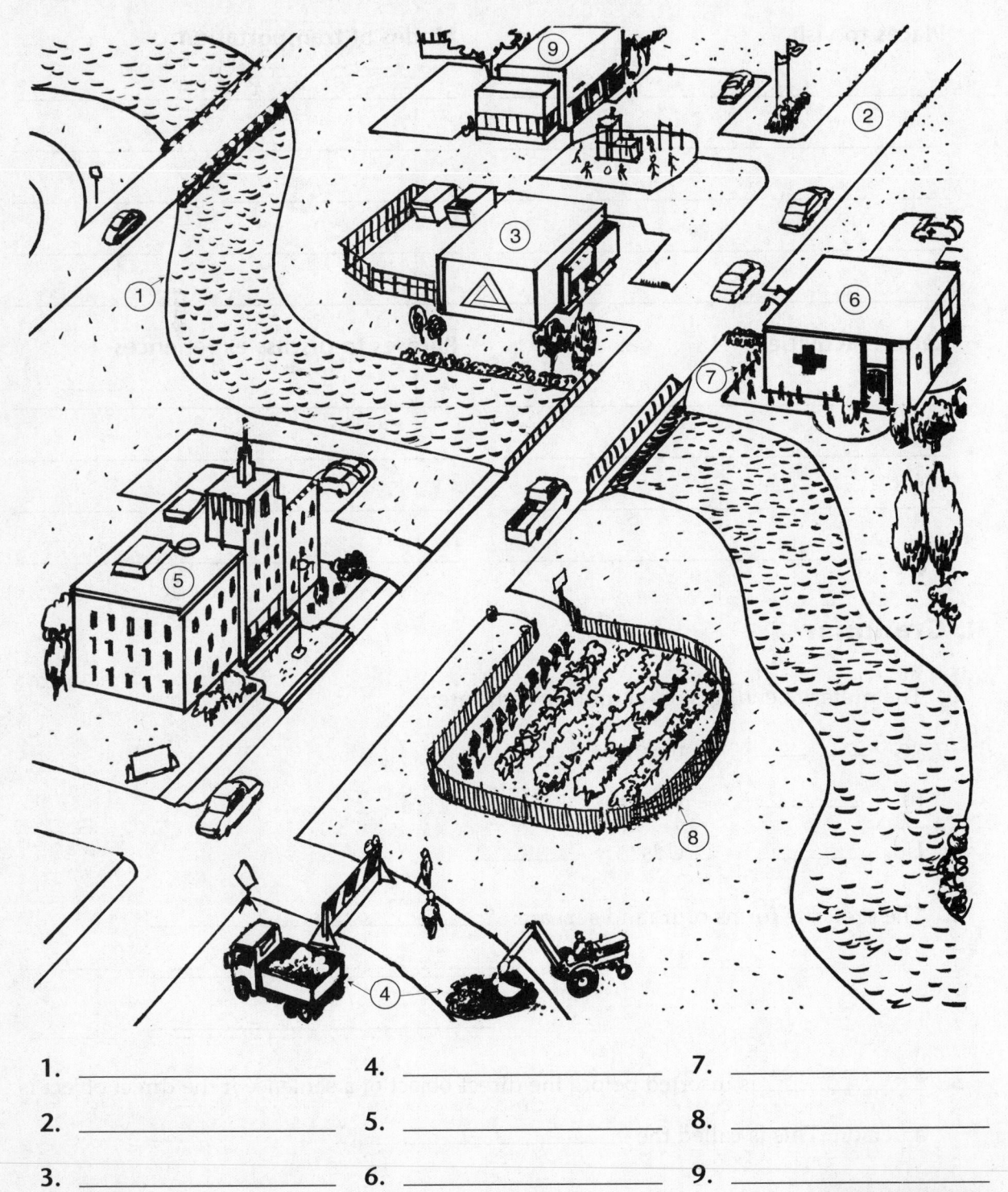

1. _____   4. _____   7. _____

2. _____   5. _____   8. _____

3. _____   6. _____   9. _____

realidades.com
• Web Code: jcd-0811

Realidades **B**

Capítulo 8B

Nombre _____

Fecha _____

Hora _____

Core Practice **8B-2**

El reciclaje

A. Your community is starting a recycling program. Label each item below with words from your vocabulary.

1. _____

2. _____

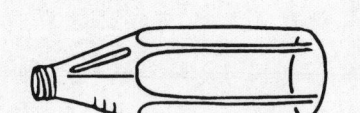

3. _____

4. _____

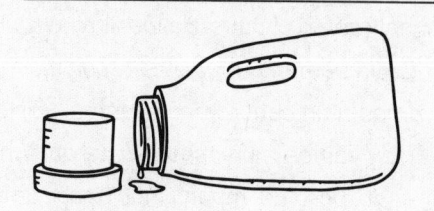

5. la botella de _____

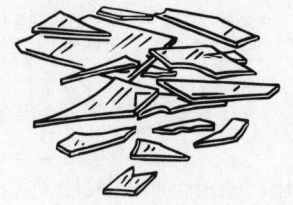

6. la botella de _____

B. Now, write sentences to say whether or not it is necessary to recycle the items below. Follow the model.

Modelo Los tomates *No es necesario reciclar los tomates.* _____

1. El helado _____

2. El plástico _____

3. El vidrio _____

4. La sala _____

5. Las latas _____

Realidades B

Capítulo 8B

Nombre _____

Fecha _____

Hora _____

Core Practice **8B–3**

El voluntario

A. Read the letter below from Álvaro, who is working as an AmeriCorps volunteer.

Querida familia:

   ¡Qué experiencia! Hacemos tantas cosas para ayudar a los demás. La semana pasada ayudamos en un proyecto de construcción con otro grupo de voluntarios. Ellos van a terminar el proyecto. Después de eso, fuimos a un centro de reciclaje. Allí aprendimos a reciclar el papel y el vidrio. También nos enseñaron cómo separar el papel normal (como el papel de los libros) de los periódicos.

   Esta semana nosotros recogimos mucha ropa usada de varias partes de la ciudad y la llevamos a un centro para pobres. Allí le dimos la ropa a la gente pobre del barrio.

   Hoy vamos a un centro para ancianos para ayudar a personas mayores. Estoy cansado, pero es importante hacer esto.

¡Hasta pronto!

Álvaro

B. Now, answer the questions below.

1. ¿Cuántas cosas hace Álvaro para ayudar a los demás? ¿Cuáles son? _____

_____

_____

_____

2. ¿Qué aprendió Álvaro en el centro de reciclaje? _____

_____

3. ¿Adónde llevaron Álvaro y los voluntarios la ropa usada? _____

_____

4. ¿A quiénes le dieron la ropa? _____

_____

5. ¿Qué hace Álvaro hoy? _____

_____

realidades.com
• Web Code: jcd-0812

Realidades **B**

Capítulo 8B

Nombre

Fecha

Hora

Core Practice **8B–4**

¿Qué haces en la comunidad?

You overhear two friends telling their teacher about what they do to help out in their communities. You can't hear what the teacher is asking. Fill in the teacher's questions. Follow the model.

Modelo   — ¿Uds. ayudan en la comunidad?

— Sí, trabajamos como voluntarios en la comunidad.

— ¿_____?

— Trabajamos en una escuela primaria. Les enseñamos a los niños a leer.

— ¿_____?

— También recogemos ropa usada.

— ¿_____?

— Recogemos la ropa usada del barrio.

— ¿_____?

— Hay que separar la ropa y después lavarla.

— ¿_____?

— Le damos la ropa usada a la gente pobre del barrio.

— ¿_____?

— Sí, ayudamos en el hospital.

— ¿_____?

— Trabajamos como voluntarios en un hospital para niños. Nos encanta el trabajo voluntario.

Realidades **B**

Capítulo 8B

Nombre _____

Fecha _____

Hora _____

Core Practice **8B–5**

¿Quién dice qué?

The people in the chart below are concerned citizens. Tell what each says by combining the subject on the left with the phrase on the right using **decir** + **que**. Follow the model.

Subjects	Phrases
Smokey the Bear	Hay que tener cuidado en el campamento.
Los directores del centro de reciclaje	Es necesario separar el plástico y el vidrio.
Gloria	La gente tiene que limpiar el barrio.
Yo	Todos deben participar en las actividades de la comunidad.
La profesora	Es esencial hacer trabajo voluntario.
La Cruz Roja	Es importante ayudar a los enfermos.
Tú	Es importante llevar la ropa usada a centros para los pobres.
Mi familia y yo	Es importante reciclar las botellas y latas.

Modelo *Smokey the Bear dice que hay que tener cuidado en el campamento.*

1. _____

2. _____

3. _____

4. _____

5. _____

6. _____

7. _____

realidades.com
• Web Code: jcd-0813

Realidades Ⓑ

Capítulo 8B

Nombre _____

Fecha _____

Hora _____

Core Practice **8B–6**

Más trabajo voluntario

A. Write the indirect object pronouns that correspond to the following phrases.

1. A Javier y a Sara _____
2. A Diego y a mí _____
3. A la Dra. Estes _____
4. A Uds. _____
5. A Tito _____

6. A Luz y a ti _____
7. A ti _____
8. A nosotros _____
9. Al Sr. Pérez _____
10. A mí _____

B. Now, fill in the blanks in the following sentences with the correct indirect object pronouns.

1. La Cruz Roja _____ ayuda a las personas de la comunidad.

2. Nuestros padres _____ hablaron a mi hermano y a mí del reciclaje.

3. Mi profesora _____ ayudó a decidir qué trabajo voluntario me gustaría hacer.

4. _____ dice el profesor al estudiante que es importante separar las latas y el plástico.

5. Las personas _____ escriben al director del centro de reciclaje para recibir información sobre el reciclaje.

6. ¿Tus padres _____ dicen que debes ayudar a los demás?

7. _____ traigo unos juguetes a los niños en el hospital.

8. Los ancianos están muy contentos cuando _____ decimos que volvemos mañana.

Realidades B

Capítulo 8B

Nombre _____

Fecha _____

Hora _____

Core Practice **8B–7**

¿Hacer o dar?

A. Fill in the chart below with the correct forms of **hacer** and **dar** in the preterite.

	HACER	DAR
yo	*hice*	*di*
tú		
él, ella, Ud.		
nosotros		
vosotros	*hicisteis*	*disteis*
ellos, ellas, Uds.		

B. Now, fill in the blanks in the telephone conversation below with the appropriate forms from the chart above.

LEYDIN: ¡Mamá, estoy aquí en los Estados Unidos!

MADRE: Hola, hija. ¿Cómo estás?

LEYDIN: Bien, mamá. Yo _____ muchas cosas ayer después de llegar.

MADRE: ¿Qué _____?

LEYDIN: Pues, primero les _____ los regalos a toda la familia.

MADRE: ¿Y la abuelita te _____ un regalo a ti, también?

LEYDIN: Sí, ¡una bicicleta nueva! Estoy muy contenta.

MADRE: Y, ¿qué _____ Uds. después?

LEYDIN: Los primos _____ la tarea y la abuelita y yo le _____ la lista

de cosas que comprar para la cena. Después le _____ la lista al abuelo,

quien _____ las compras en el supermercado.

MADRE: ¿_____ Uds. algo más?

LEYDIN: Sí. Después de comer, yo _____ un postre especial para todos: ¡tu

famoso pastel de tres leches!

MADRE: ¡Qué coincidencia! Yo _____ uno también y les _____ un

poco a nuestros amigos, los Sánchez. ¿Qué más . . .?

• Web Code: jcd-0814

Realidades **B**

Capítulo 8B

Nombre _____

Hora _____

Fecha _____

Core Practice **8B-8**

Repaso

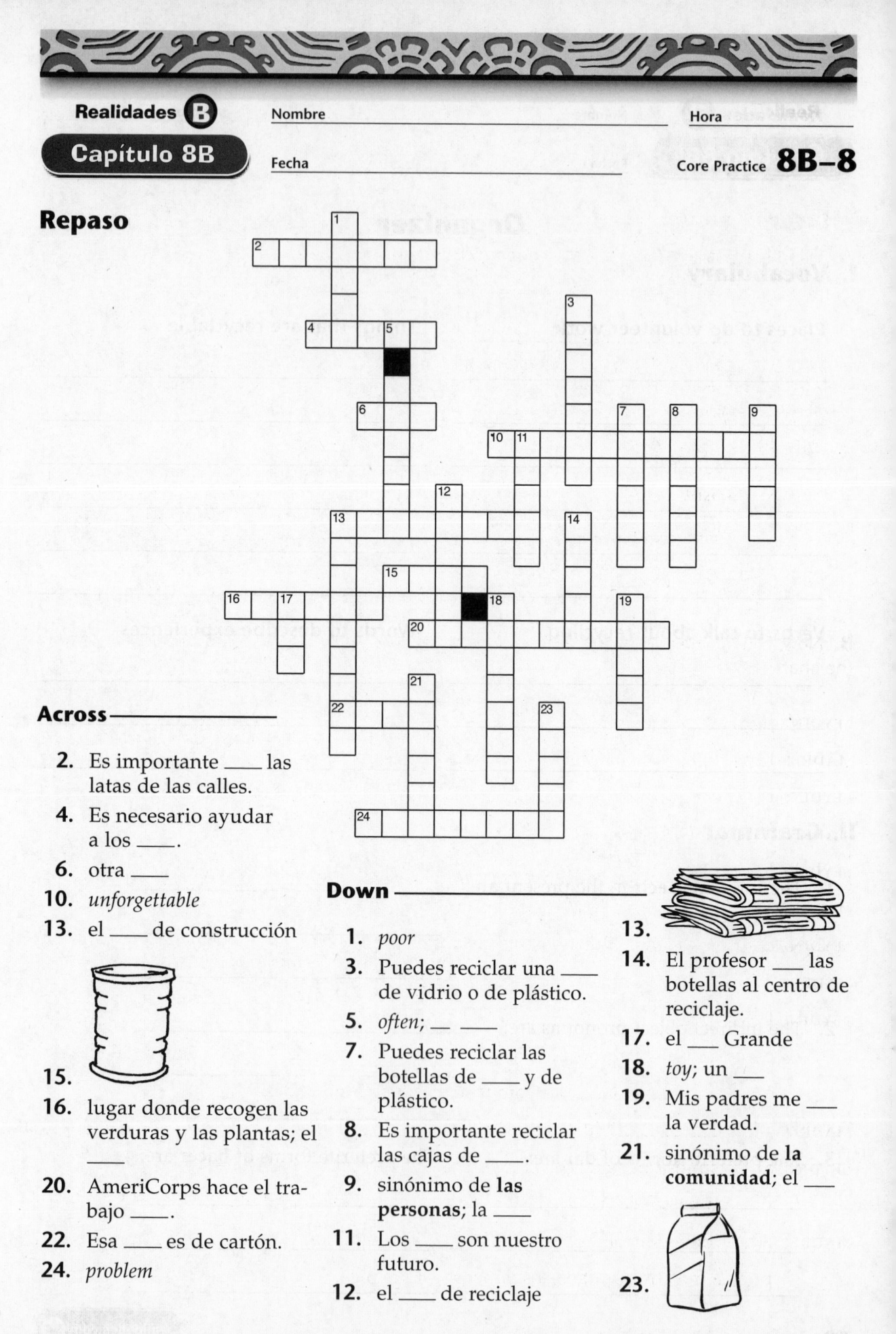

Across

2. Es importante ____ las latas de las calles.

4. Es necesario ayudar a los ____.

6. otra ____

10. *unforgettable*

13. el ____ de construcción

15.

16. lugar donde recogen las verduras y las plantas; el ____

20. AmeriCorps hace el trabajo ____.

22. Esa ____ es de cartón.

24. *problem*

Down

1. *poor*

3. Puedes reciclar una ____ de vidrio o de plástico.

5. *often*; __ ____

7. Puedes reciclar las botellas de ____ y de plástico.

8. Es importante reciclar las cajas de ____.

9. sinónimo de **las personas**; la ____

11. Los ____ son nuestro futuro.

12. el ____ de reciclaje

13.

14. El profesor ____ las botellas al centro de reciclaje.

17. el ____ Grande

18. *toy*; un ____

19. Mis padres me ____ la verdad.

21. sinónimo de **la comunidad**; el ____

23.

Realidades B

Capítulo 8B

Nombre _____

Fecha _____

Hora _____

Core Practice **8B–9**

Organizer

I. Vocabulary

Places to do volunteer work

_____

_____

_____

_____

_____

Things that are recyclable

_____

_____

_____

_____

_____

Verbs to talk about recycling

_____

_____

_____

Words to describe experiences

_____

_____

_____

II. Grammar

1. The forms of **decir** in the present are: _____ _____

   _____ _____

   _____ _____

2. The indirect object pronouns are: _____ _____

   _____ _____

   _____ _____

3. The preterite forms of **dar** are:

   _____ _____ _____

   _____ _____ _____

   _____ _____ _____

   The preterite forms of **hacer** are:

   _____ _____

   _____ _____

   _____ _____

realidades.com

• Web Code: jcd-0817

Realidades **B**

Capítulo 9A

Nombre _____

Fecha _____

Hora _____

Core Practice **9A–1**

Las películas

A. You love movies, but always forget to check the newspaper for the showings. You constantly have to ask your friends what movies are showing and at what time. Complete each dialogue by filling in the words that best identify the picture.

1. — ¿Cuándo empieza la _____?

   — Empieza a las nueve y media. Son casi las nueve. ¡Vamos ahora!

2. — ¿Va a ser larga la _____?

   — Sí. Empieza a las dos y media y termina a las cinco menos cuarto.

3. — ¿A qué hora dan la _____?

   — A las seis.

4. — ¿Cuánto dura el _____?

   — Dura menos de tres horas.

5. — ¿Cuándo va a empezar la _____?

   — Empieza a las cuatro y media.

6. — Ya es la una y veinte. ¿Qué podemos hacer?

   — Podemos ir al cine a ver una _____

B. Now, say the following time expressions another way using new vocabulary phrases.

1. Son las cinco menos diez. _____.

2. Son las dos y treinta. _____.

3. Dura una hora y cincuenta minutos. Dura _____.

4. Termina a las once y cuarenta. Termina _____.

Realidades B

Capítulo 9A

Nombre _____

Hora _____

Fecha _____

Core Practice **9A–2**

¿Qué programas les gustan?

Read the information about each person below. Then decide which TV program would be best for him or her and write it in the blank.

1. Pedro es gracioso. Siempre cuenta chistes y hace cosas cómicas. A él le gustan

   los programas _____.

2. Mi padre lee el periódico todos los días. Le interesa la política. A él le gustan

   los programas _____.

3. La profesora tiene dos hijos y quiere enseñarles mucho. También busca información

   para usar en la clase. Ella prefiere los programas _____.

4. Abuela no trabaja y tiene que estar en casa. Le interesan mucho los

   juegos, especialmente cuando la gente gana dinero. A ella le gustan los programas

   _____.

5. Javi toca la guitarra y Juanita canta. Pasan casi todo el tiempo practicando la

   música. A ellos les gustan los programas _____.

6. Rosa estudia inglés. Un día quiere trabajar para un periódico. Para aprender más

   de la gente, ella ve los programas _____.

7. Ronaldo es deportista. Juega al fútbol, al béisbol y al básquetbol. Cuando no está

   practicando un deporte está viendo programas _____.

8. A Cristina le gustan las historias. Lee novelas románticas y a veces escribe cuentos

   de amor. A ella le gustan las _____.

realidades.com

• Web Code: jcd-0901

Realidades (B)

Capítulo 9A

Nombre _____

Hora _____

Fecha _____

Core Practice **9A–3**

¿Cómo son las cosas allí?

Luzma is writing a letter to her pen pal in the U.S. She is telling her pen pal about TV and movies in her country. Fill in the blanks with the words that best complete her thoughts.

Querida Valerie,

    ¿Qué tal? ¿Cómo fue la _____ que viste la semana pasada? En

mi país me encanta ir al cine. Me gustan más las películas _____ .

Mi hermano es policía y _____ yo sé mucho _____

los policías. También me interesa esta clase de películas porque son más

_____ que una comedia o la ciencia ficción. Las comedias

_____ aburren y a veces son infantiles. No me gustan las películas

de _____ porque son demasiado violentas. ¿Qué _____

película te gusta más a ti?

    Ahora te hablo de los _____ de televisión aquí. Bueno, no son

muy diferentes de los programas de allí. Tenemos programas de dibujos

animados como *Rin, ran, run*, programas de _____ como *¡Una*

fortuna para ti! y tenemos las noticias. Yo veo las noticias pero sólo me

interesan los programas que dan sobre la policía en el _____ 56.

    Eso es todo. Adiós, amiga.

Luzma

Realidades **B**

Capítulo 9A

Nombre _____

Fecha _____

Hora _____

Core Practice **9A–4**

Tus programas favoritos

Read the TV listings below, then answer the questions that follow in complete sentences.

EVENING — NOCHE

6PM **2** Noticias
  18 Amigos
  26 Noticias
  30 Pepito y Paquito
  33 Mi casa
  42 Deportivas
  60 Música cubana
7pm **2** Los monos
  18 Noticias
  26 Entre tú y yo
  30 Noticias
  33 Noticias
  42 Deportes
  60 La salsa y la samba

8PM **2** ¡Niágara!
  18 Amigos
  26 Película: El monstruo verde
  30 El mundo real
  33 Hoy día
  42 Fútbol . . . .
  60 ¿Puedes cantar?
9PM **2** El zoológico
  18 Mi Amiga Sara
  26 . . . .
  30 El día en Alaska
  33 ¡Ganar un coche!
  42 . . . .
  60 Baile en vivo

1. ¿Cuántos programas de noticias empiezan a las seis? _____

2. ¿Qué clase de programas tiene el canal 42? _____

   ¿Y el canal 60? _____

   ¿Y el canal 2? _____

3. ¿Qué programa deportivo puedes ver a las ocho? _____

   _____

4. Para ver un programa educativo, ¿vas a ver el canal 2 o el 18 a las nueve? _____

   _____

5. ¿Qué clase de programa empieza a las nueve en el canal 33? _____

   ¿Y a las nueve en el canal 30? _____

6. ¿Qué clase de programa dan a las siete en el canal 26? _____

7. ¿Dan una película de horror a las ocho en el canal 26? _____

   _____

• Web Code: jcd-0902

Realidades B

Capítulo 9A

Nombre _____

Hora _____

Fecha _____

Core Practice **9A–5**

Acabo de . . .

Write what the following people just finished doing and are now going to do, based on the pictures. Follow the model.

Modelo   Marta _acaba de estudiar. Ahora va a dormir._

Anabel _____

1. _____

Nosotros _____

2. _____

Ellas _____

3. _____

Yo _____

4. _____

Tú _____

5. _____

Juan y el Sr. Lebredo _____

6. _____

Roberto _____

7. _____

Ana María _____

8. _____

• Web Code: jcd-0903

Realidades **B**

Capítulo 9A

Nombre _____

Hora _____

Fecha _____

Core Practice **9A–6**

Más gustos

A. Complete the sentences below with the correct forms of the verbs given.

1. Al Presidente le _____ (interesar) la política.

2. ¡Qué terrible! Me _____ (doler) el pie izquierdo.

3. A los estudiantes les _____ (aburrir) las presentaciones largas.

4. A nosotros nos _____ (encantar) ver comedias.

5. A tus hermanos les _____ (gustar) las películas de horror.

6. A ti te _____ (interesar) el teatro.

7. Me _____ (quedar) bien los pantalones pero me

   _____ (faltar) el dinero para comprarlos.

B. Now, complete each sentence below with the correct form of the verb given and the appropriate indirect object pronoun. Follow the model.

Modelo   A Carlos _____*le aburre*_____ (aburrir) la política.

1. A mí _____ (faltar) un lápiz.

2. A ellas _____ (aburrir) las clases de arte.

3. A Carmen _____ (quedar) bien la falda, ¿no?

4. A ti _____ (encantar) los programas deportivos.

5. ¿A ti y a Pedro _____ (gustar) leer revistas?

6. A mi papá _____ (doler) los pies.

7. ¿A Ud. _____ (faltar) los cuadernos?

8. A nosotros _____ (interesar) las obras de teatro.

9. A Lola y a Roberto _____ (interesar) el programa musical y el programa educativo.

• Web Code: jcd-0904

Realidades **B**

Capítulo 9A

Nombre _____

Fecha _____

Hora _____

Core Practice **9A–7**

Frases revueltas

The following sentences are mixed up. Rearrange them so that they are grammatically correct and make sense. Don't forget to conjugate verbs where appropriate. Follow the model.

Modelo ir al cine / me / a mí / y al centro comercial / gustar

A mí me gusta ir al cine y al centro comercial.

1. le / leer / a Elena / poemas / encantar / y escribir

   _____

2. negros / unos zapatos / te / para / faltar / a ti / ir a la fiesta

   _____

3. diez kilómetros / a mí / doler / después de / me / los pies / correr

   _____

4. al Sr. Mirabal / interesar / americano / le / el fútbol

   _____

5. los programas / les / a mis padres / de entrevistas / aburrir

   _____

6. importar / voluntario / a nosotros / el trabajo / nos

   _____

7. a Uds. / los boletos para el cine / les / para comprar / faltar / el dinero

   _____

8. interesar / les / a José y a Felipe / policíacas / las películas

   _____

9. el trabajo / a Angélica / aburrir / le

   _____

10. la comida / italiana / encantar / a Vanessa y a mí / nos

    _____

Realidades **B**

Capítulo 9A

Nombre _____

Fecha _____

Hora _____

Core Practice **9A–8**

Repaso

Down ─────────────

1. Yo veo mis programas favoritos en el ____ cinco.

2. Es más que interesante; es ____.

4. *already*

5. No es actor, es ____.

7. No es interesante, es ____.

9. Me van a ____ zapatos. Necesito comprarlos.

10. Puedes leer las ____ o verlas en la tele.

11. ____ película ____

14. *really?*

16. A Paco le gusta el fútbol. Ve programas ____.

18. No sé mucho ____ eso.

Across ─────────────

3. Cuando vas al cine, ves una ____.

6.

8. un programa en la tele que cuenta las historias románticas de la gente; la ____

12. *therefore*

13. Una comedia es ____.

15. No es actriz, es ____.

16. Los programas ____ una hora.

17. *Entre tú y yo* es un programa de ____.

19. Cuando la gente gana dinero, es un programa de ____.

Organizer

I. Vocabulary

Types of television programs

_____

_____

_____

_____

_____

_____

Types of movies

_____

_____

_____

_____

_____

_____

Words to describe movies/programs

_____

_____

_____

_____

_____

_____

Words to express opinions

_____

_____

_____

_____

_____

_____

II. Grammar

1. Use _____ + _____ to say what you or others have just finished doing.

2. **Me gusta** is literally translated as "_____." So, the construction is formed by putting the _____ first, followed by the _____ , and finally the _____ .

Realidades B

Capítulo 9B

Nombre _____

Fecha _____

Hora _____

Core Practice **9B–1**

El laboratorio

Label the computer lab below with the appropriate words.

1. _____   4. _____

2. _____   5. _____

3. _____   6. _____

Realidades B

Capítulo 9B

Nombre _____

Hora _____

Fecha _____

Core Practice **9B–2**

Las asociaciones

Write the words from your vocabulary that you associate with each of the following definitions.

1. Una sala de clases con muchas computadoras   _____

2. Lugar para hablar con otras personas en línea   _____

3. Comunicarse con otros por computadora   _____

4. Lo que haces si quieres aprender más   _____

5. Buscar información   _____

6. Un lugar de la Red dedicado a algún tema   _____

7. Hacer actividades electrónicas divertidas   _____

8. Una comunicación *no* por correo electrónico   _____

9. Una carta que envías para una fecha especial   _____

10. Expresar y comprender ideas de otra persona   _____

11. Si quieres hacer un disco compacto   _____

12. Un artista puede hacerlos en la computadora   _____

Realidades Ⓑ

Capítulo 9B

Nombre _____

Hora _____

Fecha _____

Core Practice **9B–3**

El sitio Web

Sara has just purchased a laptop computer. She is so excited that she just has to tell her friend Ramón. In the e-mail below write the words that best complete her thoughts.

Ramón,

Ay, amigo, tienes que comprarte una computadora

_____. ¡Son los mejores juguetes del mundo!

Cuando vas de vacaciones puedes llevarla en tu mochila y

cuando estás en el hotel puedes _____ en la

Red, escribir por _____ o

_____ información de la Red. ¿Y quieres

sacar fotos? Con una cámara _____ puedes

sacarlas y ponerlas en la computadora. También puedes

mandar las fotos a otra _____electrónica

si quieres. ¿Qué te _____? ¿Es difícil?

Puedes _____ un curso para aprender más

sobre cómo usar esta clase de cámara y cómo crear

_____ en la computadora. No debes tener

_____ de buscar información sobre

cámaras digitales porque hay muchas personas que

_____ usarlas o que escribieron unos

_____ sobre estas cámaras.

Bueno, podemos hablar más de esto_____

porque no tengo tiempo ahora. Hasta luego.

Sara

realidades.com ✔
• Web Code: jcd-0912

Realidades **B**

Capítulo 9B

Nombre _____

Fecha _____

Hora _____

Core Practice **9B–4**

¡Una computadora muy buena!

Your local newspaper recently ran an ad for a new computer and many of your friends bought one. Read some of the computer's capabilities in the ad below. Then, based on the information you are given about each person that bought this computer, say what he or she uses the new computer for. Follow the model.

> ## CON LA COMPUTADORA ES POSIBLE:
>
> - Grabar un disco compacto
> - Preparar presentaciones
> - Escribir por correo electrónico
> - Usar una cámara digital
> - Visitar salones de chat
> - Navegar en la Red
> - Crear documentos
> - Estar en línea

Modelo A Juan le gusta bajar información.

Juan usa la computadora para estar en línea.

1. A Alejandro le gusta escribir cuentos y composiciones.

_____

2. A Diego le gusta sacar fotos.

_____

3. A Caridad le gusta tocar y escuchar música.

_____

4. A Ramiro le gusta buscar los sitios Web.

_____

5. A Esperanza le gusta conocer y hablar con otras personas.

_____

6. A Lucita le gusta escribir tarjetas y cartas a su familia que vive en otra ciudad.

_____

7. A Rodrigo le gusta enseñar a los niños.

_____

Realidades B

Capítulo 9B

Nombre _____

Fecha _____

Hora _____

Core Practice **9B–5**

¿Pedir o servir?

A. Fill in the charts below with the present tense forms of the verbs **pedir** and **servir**.

	PEDIR	SERVIR
yo	*pido*	
tú		
él, ella, Ud.		*sirve*
nosotros		
vosotros	*pedís*	*servís*
ellos, ellas, Uds.		

B. Complete the mini-conversations below with the correct forms of **pedir** or **servir**.

1. — Cuando vas al restaurante Marino para comer, ¿qué _____ tú?

   — Normalmente _____ una ensalada y una pasta.

2. — ¿Para qué _____ esto?

   — _____ para grabar discos compactos, hijo.

3. — ¿Los camareros les _____ rápidamente en el restaurante Guzmán?

   — Sí, son muy trabajadores.

4. — No puedo ver esos gráficos.

   — (Nosotros) _____ ayuda, entonces.

5. — Bienvenida a la fiesta. ¿Le _____ algo?

   — Sí, un refresco, por favor.

6. — Vamos al restaurante. Esta noche ellos _____ pollo con salsa y pasta.

   — Yo siempre _____ el pollo.

7. — ¿Para qué _____ el menú?

   — _____ para conocer la comida del restaurante. ¿Y qué vas a

   _____ del menú?

   — Yo siempre _____ la misma cosa. . . el bistec.

realidades.com
• Web Code: jcd-0913

Realidades B

Capítulo 9B

Nombre _____

Fecha _____

Hora _____

Core Practice **9B–6**

¿Saber o conocer?

A. Write either **saber** or **conocer** in the blanks under the items below.

1. Mi número de teléfono
   _____

2. Usar una computadora
   _____

3. El profesor de la clase de español
   _____

4. La película *Casablanca*
   _____

5. Leer música
   _____

6. La ciudad de Nueva York
   _____

7. Mi madre
   _____

8. Tu mejor amigo
   _____

9. Navegar en la Red
   _____

10. El sitio Web
   _____

B. Fill in the missing forms of **saber** and **conocer** in the charts below.

	SABER	CONOCER
yo		
tú		
él, ella, Ud.	sabe	conoce
nosotros		
vosotros	sabéis	conocéis
ellos, ellas, Uds.		

C. Complete the following sentences using the correct forms of **saber** or **conocer**.

1. Juan, ¿ _____ la fecha de hoy?

2. ¿Alguien _____ a un médico bueno?

3. Mis padres _____ bailar muy bien.

4. Nosotros _____ todas las palabras de la obra.

5. ¿ _____ dónde está el Museo del Prado?

realidades.com
• Web Code: jcd-0914

Realidades **B**

Capítulo 9B

Nombre _____

Fecha _____

Hora _____

Core Practice **9B–7**

Planes para la noche

The Miranda family is planning to go out to eat. Fill in their conversation using forms of
conocer, saber, pedir, or **servir.**

PADRE: Vamos al restaurante Vista del Mar. ¿Lo _____ Uds.? Me gusta

mucho.

TERESA: Yo no lo _____ pero _____ dónde está. ¡Quiero ir

a ese restaurante!

TOMÁS: Por supuesto que _____ dónde está, Tere, el nombre es Vista del Mar.

TERESA: Sí. ¿_____ Uds. que tienen el mejor pescado de la ciudad?

Es muy sabroso.

MADRE: ¿Y ellos _____ otra comida también?

TERESA: Yo no _____ . ¿Sabes tú, Tomás?

TOMÁS: Sí. Allí _____ mucha comida rica.

PADRE: Yo _____ el pescado porque me encanta.

TOMÁS: Sí, me encanta el pescado también.

TERESA: Es verdad Tomás, pero siempre _____ la misma cosa cuando

comemos pescado.

PADRE: Por eso vamos a este restaurante. Puedes _____ de todo y va a ser

sabrosísimo.

TERESA: ¡Yo quiero _____ ese restaurante!

MADRE: Pues, estamos de acuerdo. Vamos a Vista del Mar.

realidades.com

• Web Code: jcd-0915

Realidades B

Capítulo 9B

Nombre

Hora

Fecha

Core Practice **9B–8**

Repaso

Down

1.
2. El cliente ___ un té helado porque tiene calor.
3. Voy a visitar Nueva York porque quiero ___ la.
4. ___ un disco compacto
6. Los estudiantes hacen un ___ del presidente Lincoln.
8. Quiero escribirte una carta. ¿Cuál es tu ___ electrónica?
9. Yo escribo por ___ electrónico.
11. Estoy en línea. Quiero ___ en ___.
12. *song*; la ___
13. El ___ Web para este libro es **realidades.com.**
14. No tengo ese programa. Lo voy a ___ de la Red.
16. Necesito ___ información para mi informe.
18. La artista sabe muy bien hacer ___ en la computadora.
19. Necesito una computadora que puede ___ documentos.
21. *slide*; la ___

Across

1. Quiero ___ un curso.
5. No debes tener ___ de la tecnología.
7. Para navegar en la Red, hay que estar ___ ___.
10. Si quieres hablar con personas inmediatamente, vas a un ___ de chat.
13. ¿Para qué ___?
15. *to communicate (with)*
17. Mi amiga me escribió una ___.
20. No me gusta hablar por teléfono. Me gusta hablar ___ _ _.
22. Voy a la escuela porque quiero ___ cómo hacer cosas.
23. Vamos al ___ para usar las computadoras de la escuela.
24. la computadora ___

Nombre _____

Fecha _____

Hora _____

Core Practice **9B–9**

Organizer

I. Vocabulary

Words to talk about the Web

_____

_____

_____

Words to name other electronics

_____

_____

_____

Verbs related to online activities

_____

_____

_____

_____

II. Grammar

1. The present tense of **pedir** is:

_____   _____

_____   _____

_____   _____

The present tense of **servir** is:

_____   _____

_____   _____

_____   _____

2. Use the verb _____ for information or activities that you know. Use

the verb _____ to talk about familiarity with people, places, or things.